The Scandal of the Gospel

"Chuck Campbell always takes us deeper in his writings: deeper theologically, deeper biblically, deeper homiletically. This book is no exception. He delves into the grotesque scandal that is at the heart of the Christian gospel, demonstrates how it has been used for good and for evil, and challenges us to engage it deeply—for goodness' sake—in our own preaching. Out of the shallows and into deep, disorienting preaching waters he calls us. Enter at your own risk!"

—LEONORA TUBBS TISDALE, Clement-Muehl Professor
Emerita of Divinity (Homiletics), Yale Divinity School

"With the *The Scandal of the Gospel*, Campbell breaks new ground and suggests alternative paths for the future of homiletics. Through its analyses of the relationship between preaching and the grotesque, from the carnivalesque, incarnate Word through first-century grottos to contemporary literature and the climate crisis, this book will simultaneously unsettle and liberate its readers."

—MARLENE RINGGAARD LORENSEN, Professor of
Practical Theology, University of Copenhagen

"This gorgeous theological treatment of the grotesque gospel demonstrates once again why Charles L. Campbell is one of the most liberative homileticians of our time. If you want to be freed from easy closed-off homiletical answers, pulpit clichés, and neat sermon patterns, this book is for you. It will embolden you to confront the dehumanizing and destructive powers that weaponize the grotesque in the world and challenge you to become more human, more creaturely, and more compassionate, especially toward the other, including creation as a whole. Moreover, this provocative, imaginative, generative work will lead readers to the borderlands of creation where Jesus, the grotesque God, can be found. What a beautiful literary expression of a Word before the powers!"

—LUKE A. POWERY, Dean, Duke University Chapel; and
Associate Professor of Homiletics, Duke Divinity School

"Charles Campbell is one of the most original thinkers in the field of preaching. He always advances our thought by first knocking it off balance, and this book is no exception. Here he allows the shadowy light of the grotesque to fall across the pulpit, exposing the all-too-shiny empty hopes, the all-too-tidy resolutions, and all-too-easy faux resurrections of much of today's preaching. Campbell guides us toward a preaching that is more honest, more alert, more porous to the wild interactions of such forces as poetry, raw experience, unresolved plots, punk protests, and jazz. This is an unforgettable book."

—THOMAS G. LONG, Bandy Professor Emeritus of
Preaching, Candler School of Theology of Emory University

"Charles Campbell steers us away from some of the cherished formulas that have grounded Christian preaching, and he urges us to embrace an edgier, more grotesque approach. He unveils a pathbreaking vision of preaching that reckons with the horrors of the current moment and yet remains faithful to the gospel. This book crackles with electricity and will resonate with preachers, poets, and other truth-tellers. A new era in homiletics has begun."

—DONYELLE C. MCCRAY, Associate Professor of
Homiletics, Yale Divinity School

"I don't have words to express how extraordinary I believe this book is. It cracks the teaching of preaching wide open. It's an exercise in homiletical imagination, and it will require of us pedagogical acts of imagination that go way beyond anything we may have tried or thought appropriate. Faithful preaching of a grotesque gospel requires careful description of complex human lives—description of lives we believe God has entered, not tidy resolutions or neat homiletical patterns. *The Scandal of the Gospel* explores a more extreme homiletic—one that disrupts theology and homiletics in valuable ways and that recognizes and resists the weaponized grotesque."

—ANNA CARTER FLORENCE, Peter Marshall Professor of
Preaching, Columbia Theological Seminary

The Scandal of the Gospel

Preaching and the Grotesque

Charles L. Campbell

© 2021 Charles L. Campbell
Foreword © 2021 Westminster John Knox Press

First edition
Published by Westminster John Knox Press
Louisville, Kentucky

21 22 23 24 25 26 27 28 29—10 9 8 7 6 5 4 3 2 1

All rights reserved. No part of this book may be reproduced or transmitted in any form or by any means, electronic or mechanical, including photocopying, recording, or by any information storage or retrieval system, without permission in writing from the publisher. For information, address Westminster John Knox Press, 100 Witherspoon Street, Louisville, Kentucky 40202-1396. Or contact us online at www.wjkbooks.com.

Scripture quotations are from the New Revised Standard Version of the Bible, copyright © 1989 by the Division of Christian Education of the National Council of the Churches of Christ in the U.S.A., and are used by permission. In this book, Scripture may be paraphrased or summarized.

"Upon Waking" from *The Devil's Workshop*, by Demetria Martinez. © 2002 The Arizona Board of Regents. Reprinted by permission of the University of Arizona Press. Lucille Clifton, "why some people be mad at me sometimes," from *The Collected Poems of Lucille Clifton.* Copyright © 1987 by Lucille Clifton. Reprinted with the permission of The Permissions Company, LLC on behalf of BOA Editions Ltd., www.boaeditions.org. Anna Akhmatova, "Instead of a Preface," from "Requiem" from *Complete Poems of Anna Akhmatova*, translated by Judith Hemschemeyer, edited and introduced by Roberta Reeder. Copyright © 1989, 1992, 1997 by Judith Hemschemeyer. Reprinted with the permission of The Permissions Company, LLC on behalf of Zephyr Press, www.zephyrpress.org. Permission to use Anna Akhmatova's "Instead of a Preface" is also granted by Canongate Books.

Book design by Sharon Adams
Cover design by Barbara LeVan Fisher, www.levanfisherdesign.com
Cover art: The Red Christ, 1922 (oil on canvas), Corinth, Lovis
(Franz Heinrich Louis) (1858–1925)

Library of Congress Cataloging-in-Publication Data

Names: Campbell, Charles L., 1954- author.
Title: The scandal of the gospel : preaching and the grotesque / Charles L. Campbell.
Description: First edition. | Louisville, Kentucky : Westminster John Knox Press, [2021] | Includes bibliographical references and index. | Summary: "Examines the theological, homiletical, and social implications of a grotesque gospel for contemporary preachers. It is the written adaptation of Yale Divinity School's Beecher Lectures, given by Charles Campbell in 2018"-- Provided by publisher.
Identifiers: LCCN 2021033996 (print) | LCCN 2021033997 (ebook) | ISBN 9780664266202 (paperback) | ISBN 9781646982202 (ebook)
Subjects: LCSH: Bible. New Testament--Homiletical use. | Preaching. | Bible. New Testament--Criticism, interpretation, etc. | Grotesque--Biblical teaching.
Classification: LCC BS2361.3 .C36 2021 (print) | LCC BS2361.3 (ebook) | DDC 251--dc23
LC record available at https://lccn.loc.gov/2021033996
LC ebook record available at https://lccn.loc.gov/2021033997

Most Westminster John Knox Press books are available at special quantity discounts when purchased in bulk by corporations, organizations, and special-interest groups. For more information, please email SpecialSales@wjkbooks.com.

For Dana

I believe that "closure" is a steaming load of middle-class horseshite invented to pay for shrinks' Jags.
    —*Detective Frank Mackey*
        in Tana French's Faithful Place

Contents

Foreword	ix
Preface	xiii
Acknowledgments	xvii

1. Jesus in the Grotto: The Gospel as Grotesque   1
    The Gospel as Grotesque
    Preaching a Grotesque Gospel

2. The Thing: Resisting the Weaponized Grotesque   17
    Resisting the Weaponized Grotesque
    Preachers of the Fictional Page
    Humanizing Stories: The Preacher's Dilemma
    Jesus, the Man That Was a Thing

3. Incarnate Word: Preaching and the Carnivalesque Grotesque   41
    Grotesque Realism
    The Grotesque Body
    Preaching, Homiletics, and the Grotesque Body

4. Apocalypse Now: Preaching and the Environmental Grotesque   59
    Apocalypse Now
    Preaching and the Environmental Grotesque
       Who Knows? Grotesque Hope
    Environmental Justice: Resisting the Weaponized Grotesque
    Back to the Grotto: The Environmental Grotesque Body

Selected Bibliography	81
Index	87

Foreword

*H*eavy lifting. That's what preaching is. Those who deny this fact are lying to themselves and everyone else. Teaching preaching is the heaviest lifting in the academy. Almost everyone in the academy denies this, which means almost everyone is lying to themselves and to a watching world. If we take just the sheer volume and density of the work for a preacher—wrestling each week with difficult texts in order to offer a word from God that is bound up with and yet aimed at the cacophony of voices, the myriad of struggles, and the forest of feelings, dreams, and memories that weave together a congregation—it rushes us into exhaustion. If we take just the sheer volume and density of the work for a teacher of preaching—listening to hundreds of sermons over countless hours, reviewing the exegesis and interpretation of each one, cutting through the denials of the complexities of life, of the text, and of the preachers themselves—it pushes exhaustion toward madness.

There are preaching pretenders. There are those who, when faced with the heavy lifting and the exhaustion that awaits, opt out. Like those reluctant souls who go to the gym but spend most of their time walking around talking to people, never breaking a sweat, these pretenders preach lite. Easy does it. Say a few words—sound like a television commercial that glides along our waking consciousness softly touching our attention. This will not do for hard-core instructors in preaching. They war against the pretenders, aiming to kill them in all would-be preachers. "Pick up the damn weight!" This is the unspoken motto of the preaching professor. There is a refined cynicism in every preaching professor I know, honed over years of listening to people avoid the weight or seek to put the weight down as quickly as possible, long before the work is done. Their cynicism is a gift from God to the disciples of Jesus, especially those who are following him at a distance, having allowed too much space between his body and their own.

Charles Campbell (affectionately known as Chuck) allows no distance between Jesus' body and our own, no distance between Jesus' body and the body of the preacher, no distance between Jesus' body and the body of preaching. All of it is captured in the grotesque. Jesus is a shattering, a crumbling, a breaking, and a pulling apart of the building projects that constitute a life, a society, a religion, or even a world. Chuck knows this deeply, powerfully—this knowledge has been a signature of his writing and teaching for decades. So to turn to the grotesque was inevitable for him. What better idea captures what preaching must be in order to be of the shattering life? The idea of the grotesque in his hands is no aesthetic ploy. It is the means through which this seasoned warrior against facile preaching will teach us to see what God's overturning of the given order means for proclamation.

Chuck has always been an intellectual who is honest about what he sees, never allowing the scholarly myopia that often afflicts academics to capture him. He refuses to narrow the frames of intelligibility and legibility down to disciplinary conversations and concerns in what he writes. To see the grotesque as he does in this text is to open up our negotiation with two kinds of contradiction, one an obstacle and the other a necessity. The obstacle is the kind of contradiction that comes from hiding from the grotesque in favor of images, ideas, and narratives that paint Hallmark movie lives of faith. Such imagined dainty lives of faith exhibit a controlled messiness that will resolve itself into a tidy ending very shortly. In contrast, the grotto and the carnival hold truths that are closer to the heart of the gospel where things spill out of their appropriate form—the grotesque is unleashed in the body of Jesus. Porous and leaking, his body's energies and urgencies cover everyone who comes near him, upsetting what and who and how they understood themselves to be in this world and calling them into a new kind of experimentation of living on the edge with the Spirit and with their enemies.

But how do you preach that? Wrong question. What do you understand preaching to be once you grasp the grotesque calling? Instructor Campbell wants to lead us into that calling, which brings me to the necessary kind of contradiction: the contradiction that haunts the preacher who is constantly pulled toward a respectability politic resourced by a respectability preaching. That pull is toward a silence while speaking and a death while living—a corpse in the pulpit, weekly sanitized so as to never give off the odor of decay. Preaching is in constant struggle against this pull toward respectability and the living death that comes once we go under this current. That pull turns preachers into propagandists for nation-states, and/or plantation capitalism, and/or white supremacy, and/or patriarchy with its gender-binding normativity, and a host of other life designers working toward the pleasures of control. The pleasure of control is the source of the pull's remarkably tempting power. It moves us in the same direction as gospel light but without the light and without the freedom formed by that gospel.

This current is a riptide—much too strong to swim against. So preachers must, like all good swimmers, allow the current to pull them out into the deep water and then at the right moment cut across the current, slicing into the contradiction and showing the stark difference between following gospel light or grasping for the pleasure of control—of a life, or a relationship, or a community, or a world. It is the quest for control that has brought us to the brink of our ecological apocalypse as Chuck so powerfully articulates in these pages. The necessary contradiction in preaching (and teaching) is to inhabit pulpits and lecterns that are captured in the politics of respectability and yet to constantly disrupt those politics even as one is caught up in their currents. Preaching must do this not in order to be novel or sensational or even provocative but for the sake of the freedom that Jesus made real through his grotesque body. Meditating on the grotesque might keep preachers and preaching from losing this contradiction and then confusing gospel light for the pleasure of control.

The word here is "might" because taking the grotesque seriously requires cultivating a connection to those who have felt and yet feel a grotesquery turned against their bodies and their lives—the many peoples who fail or fall outside a politics of respectability and who could never fully actualize social uplift. Too dark, too queer, too poor, too slow, too criminalized, too unable to be able to mimic the self-sufficient white man, these folk show the body of Jesus calling us to boundary-breaking life together. Thus the meditation on the grotesque that Chuck recommends moves preaching more deeply into the social construction of grace-filled community, places where the shattering life of Jesus forms protocols for gathering and nurturing and renaming both those who have failed *and* those who have succeeded at a politics of respectability.

What is the new name that floats on respectability—riding out on its currents and then turning quickly and surfing, cutting across its massive waves, claiming the overturning that marks the grotesque, and announcing a freedom with God as the source of building life together?

Christian.

Willie James Jennings
Hamden, Connecticut

Preface

*I*t's come to this: I've been teaching preaching for right at thirty years—and I've arrived at the grotesque. The reason may be surprising. I've arrived at this point not because the thousands of sermons I've listened to have *been* grotesque. Rather, I've arrived here because the sermons have usually not taken the grotesque seriously enough. The pulpit, it seems, tends not simply to neglect the grotesque, but actively to resist it. I'm curious about that.

I have done this myself—not only in my preaching, but in my writing. For many years now I have focused on the folly of the gospel. I've spent more hours than I probably should have studying holy fools and jesters and tricksters and carnival. The whole time the language and imagery of the grotesque have been there. Taunting me. Troubling me. But I've avoided the grotesque. Resisted it. It seemed too shocking, too unnerving—not to mention far too huge to tackle, rearing its head as it does in virtually every area of art and life. So I just stuck with foolishness. It was less disturbing and much more fun. But the words of classical pianist Hélène Grimaud have unsettled me. In a magazine article I read awhile back, she said she admired "the more extreme players . . . people who wouldn't be afraid to play their conception to the end."[1] I have realized that folly is not the end. Indeed, it seems to me now that folly can be a way of sanitizing the grotesque—and the gospel—making them both less scandalous, more palatable. It's time to explore a more extreme homiletic.

My work on foolishness was inspired by Paul's affirmation in 1 Corinthians 1:23, where the apostle affirms that the message of Christ crucified is *both* foolishness and a *scandal* (stumbling block). But just as I resisted the grotesque in my focus on folly, I also neglected the radical scandal of the gospel. So in these chapters I am seeking

---

1. Quoted in D. T. Max, "Her Way: A Pianist of Strong Opinions," *New Yorker*, October 31, 2011, https://www.newyorker.com/magazine/2011/11/07/her-way-d-t-max.

to address aspects of the gospel that I have avoided by exploring the scandal of the gospel through the lens of the grotesque. I'm making, in Karl Barth's phrase, a "provisional attempt" to explore the implications for preaching of a scandalously grotesque gospel.[2]

The essays are an exercise in homiletical imagination.[3] I'm simply trying to make some homiletical connections between preaching and the grotesque. To paraphrase from Billy Collins's well-known poem "Introduction to Poetry," I'm wandering around in the dark room of the grotesque feeling the walls for a light switch. I'm placing my ear against the beehive of the grotesque to discover what I hear—or if I get stung. I'm dropping myself into the maze of the grotesque and trying to probe my way out, which, I've discovered, is actually impossible.[4] This is what homileticians do. We wander and explore, trying to make creative connections that help us enter more fully into the impossible practice of preaching.

In each of the chapters I explore a facet of the grotesque and its implications for homiletics. I'm not seeking consistency or system, including in the intentionally diverse array of sources on which I draw. Expect tensions and even contradictions, for that is the character of the grotesque itself. In what follows I'm simply looking this way and that to see what appears. In chapter 1 I explore the unresolved incongruities that characterize a grotesque gospel and the implications for oversimplified homiletical patterns. I examine in chapter 2 the weaponized grotesque—the use of the grotesque to dehumanize individuals and groups of people. I explore the calling of preachers to undertake the challenging and risky task of resisting this kind of dehumanization. Chapter 3 focuses on Mikhail Bakhtin's concept of the grotesque body and the implications for preaching in the Body of Christ. Finally, in chapter 4 I return to each of the preceding facets of the grotesque in relation to the current environmental crisis.

The first three chapters are slightly revised versions of the 2018

---

2. Karl Barth, *Homiletics*, trans. Geoffrey W. Bromiley and Donald E. Daniels (Louisville, KY: Westminster/John Knox Press, 1991), 47–55, 71–75.

3. My colleague Luke Powery drew my attention to this character of the essays after reading one of the original lectures.

4. Billy Collins, "Introduction to Poetry," from *The Apple That Astonished Paris* (Fayetteville: University of Arkansas Press, 1988), 58.

Lyman Beecher Lectures that I delivered at Yale Divinity School. Out of respect for their original context, I have tried to maintain some of the oral character of the lectures even with the editing necessary for publication in print. I hope my journey through these lectures enlivens the imaginations and practices of preachers—and leads to more grotesque sermons.

Acknowledgments

I am grateful to Dean Gregory Sterling and the faculty of Yale Divinity School for the invitation to give the Lyman Beecher Lectures in 2018 and for their gracious hospitality during my time at Yale. I also want to thank everyone who attended the lectures, asked excellent questions, and offered encouraging comments.

Numerous people read some or all of the chapters and gave me constructive feedback. Thank you to Dana Campbell, Willie Jennings, Peace Lee, Marlene Ringgaard Lorensen, Donyelle McCray, Jerusha Neal, and Luke Powery. In addition, Alexander Deeg organized a doctoral seminar around the lectures at the University of Leipzig. I greatly appreciated the stimulating conversation with him and his students. I especially want to thank my friend and former Duke colleague Willie Jennings for generously taking the time to write the foreword.

I also want to thank the people at Westminster John Knox Press, particularly Daniel Braden, Michele Blum, and Julie Tonini, for all their work on this project. Once again, with kindness and professionalism, they have transformed my manuscript into a book.

The lifetime of work that lies behind these essays would not have been possible without the support of my family. As young children, Lydia and Thomas patiently endured my hours in the study. As adults, they now keep me honest with their unsettling questions and insights. I'm grateful for their honesty, integrity, and love. I also give thanks every day for over forty-four years of marriage with Dana. She has been my best editor and my most challenging conversation partner. This book would not exist without her theological wisdom and unfailing love.

Chapter 1

Jesus in the Grotto

The Gospel as Grotesque

Blackwater is an award-winning Swedish crime novel by Kerstin Ekman.[1] Early in the novel one of the central characters, Annie, endures a chaotic and ultimately horrifying day. Following a lengthy train ride and grueling bus trip, Annie arrives overheated and exhausted with her five-year-old daughter in the small village of Blackwater. She finds herself in a strange place among people she doesn't know. She's an outsider, and folks are suspicious of her. She's ill at ease from the beginning. Her lover was supposed to meet her and take her to their destination—an isolated community deep in the forest. But he never shows up, which sows its own kind of concern and confusion. So all throughout the midsummer night she wanders lost in the shadowy forest through a maze of paths, stinging insects, and tangled marshy undergrowth, always concerned about her anxious and tearful daughter. But she never finds the community. The entire experience is deeply disorienting.

After hours of wandering she suddenly comes upon a grisly murder scene. The sight makes her physically sick, and her knees buckle. As she breaks her fall, her hands land in the blood, which she instinctively wipes all over her skirt before finally washing her hands in a creek. Then she and her daughter continue wandering, lost—now under the gruesome shadow of the murder, not to mention her awareness of a killer in the area, whom she thinks she has actually seen. Her entire experience is described in excruciating detail. Even the reader becomes disoriented.

---

1. Kerstin Ekman, *Blackwater*, trans. Joan Tate (New York: Picador, 1993).

Later, because she has witnessed the murder scene, Annie is taken to a home, where she is questioned by a detective in the kitchen. Ekman writes this about the interrogation:

> For the rest of her life [Annie] was to preserve the memory of that walk. But how much of it would she have remembered if he had not forced her to describe it over and over again in that warm kitchen? There must be tangled events, illogical or utterly insane actions in all lives. To forget. They refused to allow her to forget. They forced her to bind them together into a pattern. But it was a false pattern.[2]

"But it was a false pattern." This short sentence is extraordinary in a crime novel. For, while good crime fiction may do many different things, crime novels are generally about discerning patterns. They're about solving mysteries and restoring some order.[3] As novelist Steph Cha notes, crime fiction favors "a return to order from chaos."[4] Crime novels are narratives in search of some *narrative resolution* to the crime that has disrupted the order of things. But Ekman here ironically complicates the entire genre—not to mention her own novel. The pattern the detective demanded was inadequate to Annie's experience; it was a *false pattern*. So what does that mean about the solution to the murder at the end of the novel? Is that too a *false pattern*? Is that final pattern also imposed on experiences that are too complex to be captured within a neat narrative?[5]

---

2. Ekman, *Blackwater*, 70.
3. See John Scaggs, *Crime Fiction*, New Critical Idiom (London: Routledge, 2005). As Laura Miller writes, "The mystery genre is a minuet between disruption and order. The murder sets the story in motion by introducing instability: not just the moral wrong of homicide, a horror that remains fairly notional in most crime fiction, but the violation posed by the mystery itself. Far more unbearable than the murder is the fact that we don't know who did it. . . . At the end of the novel, justice is (usually) served, but, even more satisfying, the truth is made visible and incontrovertible." See Laura Miller, "Tana French's Intimate Crime Fiction," *New Yorker*, October 3, 2016. Miller also rightly notes that French's complex crime novels often subvert this formula.
4. Quoted in John Fram, "How White Crime Writers Justified Police Brutality," *New York Times*, June 4, 2020.
5. Ekman is not alone. Another award-winning Swedish crime writer has one of her investigators reflect on the process: "We humans need to simplify things, in order to make reality more manageable. Actually, we do the same thing at the police station. Simplify, try to understand, make connections, and see patterns in the complex materials of the investigation. And maybe we also make the same mistake: attributing characteristics to people and applying models to explain events because it fits our worldview" (Camilla Grebe, *The Ice beneath Her*,

I suspect that many preachers, myself included, frequently function as rather stereotypical crime novelists. We may tolerate disruption in our sermons for a little while, but usually we're after a resolution, a restoration of order—even if that is a word of hope far off in the distance. We seek to discern a pattern, a narrative, a doctrine that will provide some clarity and structure. One of the questions we preaching teachers often ask our students is, "Where is the good news in your sermon?" It's an important question. But all too often it really means something like, "Where is the resolution?" "Where is the restoration of order?" Indeed, entire homiletical theories have been structured around a move from problem to solution, from disorientation to reorientation—from itch to scratch. And I wonder if this model hasn't become the homiletical default setting, even for purportedly more open-ended sermons. But I also wonder how often we impose *false* patterns. I wonder if the gospel and life really lend themselves neatly to many of our theological and homiletical patterns.

In her recent memoir about her experience with cancer Kate Bowler challenges the false and inadequate patterns we Christians often impose on those with serious illness. She explores many of these in the book, but the title of her memoir makes the point: *Everything Happens for a Reason and Other Lies I've Loved*.[6] That's an important reminder to preachers. Have you ever noticed, for example, how often preachers throw out the "C" word—cancer—whenever we need a seemingly horrible experience to address with the gospel? Just throw out the word, as if the experience of cancer were easily summed up in a single term. But, as Bowler reminds us, there's no such uniform thing as "cancer." Every cancer is different, every experience is

---

trans. Elizabeth Clark Wessel [New York: Ballantine, 2016], 123–24). Similarly, through her shifting narrators, Tana French repeatedly subverts the simplistic patterns we would impose on the complexities of other human lives. More generally, contemporary crime fiction sometimes moves beyond the "familiar stereotype" of the genre and "preserves the ambiguities and ambivalences of a complex society"; it can "reflect the experience of unresolved lives." See Brian Cliff, "Why Irish Crime Fiction Is in Murderously Good Health," *Irish Times*, July 25, 2018, https://www.irishtimes.com/culture/books/why-irish-crime-fiction-is-in-murderously-good-health-1.3569128; also Brian Cliff, *Irish Crime Fiction* (London: Palgrave Macmillan, 2018). Contemporary crime writers are complicating the genre and exploring issues similar to those I am raising for preaching.

6. Kate Bowler, *Everything Happens for a Reason and Other Lies I've Loved* (New York: Random House, 2018).

different. And it's doubtful that even caring pastors fully understand those experiences. The loved ones and the patients themselves may not even understand. Applying a general pattern to "cancer" from the pulpit probably results in a *false* pattern for most people.

Poet Gregory Orr shares a similar experience. When he was twelve years old he accidentally shot and killed his younger brother, Peter, while they were hunting. In the hours following the incident everyone tried to comfort him by imposing a pattern on what had happened. The Christian pattern was possibly the worst: "You should know that right now Peter is in heaven with Jesus," someone said. "It may not make sense now, but it's all part of God's plan." In response to those comments Orr felt only rage and despair. "I wanted to scream at her," he wrote in his memoir: "What's wrong with you? Didn't you see his body? Don't you know what happened? Don't you know he's dead? ... This isn't Sunday School! My brother was just killed by a bullet and I fired it. What kind of nonsense are you saying?" And that day Orr rejected conventional religion for the rest of his life. His mother also tried to comfort him by telling him that his father had once killed someone in a hunting accident. And here's what Orr writes reflecting on that: "Certainly that coincidence represented some mysterious, even supernatural pattern, but who could imagine it being a happy pattern, a pattern that showed there was a God and he cared about us humans?"[7]

False patterns. That's where the grotesque comes in. For the grotesque fundamentally disrupts our familiar patterns—patterns we often use to make sense of life. As Robert Penn Warren put it, "The grotesque is one of the most obvious forms art may take to pierce the veil of familiarity, to stab us up from the drowse of the accustomed, to make us aware of the perilous paradoxicality of life."[8] Or as Flannery O'Connor has argued, the grotesque takes us through the surface of life and pushes us toward "mystery and the unexpected." It combines wild discrepancies and creates unsettling distortions in

---

7. Gregory Orr, *The Blessing: A Memoir* (San Francisco: Council Oaks Books, 2002), 15–16.

8. Quoted in James Luther Adams and William Yates, eds., *The Grotesque in Art and Literature: Theological Reflections* (Grand Rapids: Eerdmans, 1997), xi.

order to take us to the depths of life where our previous understanding is no longer adequate.⁹

The grotesque, to put it another way, *shocks* us out of our comfortable patterns, including those many of us may rely on in the pulpit. And isn't that what the gospel does as well? Isn't that deep down the "scandal"—the *offense*—of the gospel?¹⁰ Piercing the veil of familiarity. Making us aware of the perilous paradoxicality of life. Taking us through the surface of life toward mystery and the unexpected. Shocking us out of our comfortable—and false—patterns. The scandal of the gospel may simply be that it is grotesque.

The Gospel as Grotesque

So we need to look for Jesus down in the grotto, where, according to most scholars, the concept of the grotesque actually emerged. Indeed, the term "grotesque" comes from an Italian phrase meaning "work (or painting) found in a grotto" (grotto-esque).¹¹ The reference is to grottos in ancient Roman buildings that were excavated at the end of the fifteenth century and revealed fanciful, disorienting murals.¹² The art in the grottos was radically at odds with the norms of clarity, balance, and harmony presumed to be features of a classical aesthetic.¹³ The murals instead imaged a chaotic combination of incongruous and contradictory elements: beasts were fused with animal bodies, figures like the centaur combined human and nonhuman elements, human and animal heads grew out of plants—all

---

9. Flannery O'Connor, "Some Aspects of the Grotesque in Southern Fiction," in *Mystery and Manners: Occasional Prose*, ed. Sally and Robert Fitzgerald (New York: Farrar, Straus and Giroux, 1961), 40–43.

10. David McCracken uses the terms "scandal" and "offense" interchangeably. The scandal of the gospel is that which gives offense. See *The Scandal of the Gospels: Jesus, Story, and Offense* (New York: Oxford University Press, 1994).

11. Justin D. Edwards and Rune Graulund, *Grotesque*, New Critical Idiom (London: Routledge, 2013), 5.

12. Edwards and Graulund, *Grotesque*.

13. Ewa Kuryluk, *Salome and Judas in the Cave of Sex: The Grotesque; Origins, Iconography, Techniques* (Evanston, IL: Northwestern University Press, 1987), 12; Wolfgang Kayser, *The Grotesque in Art and Literature*, trans. Ulrich Weisstein (Bloomington: University of Indiana Press, 1963), 19–21.

with a seemingly wild and uncontrolled exuberance.[14] The murals presented unsettling, disorienting *hybrids* that transgressed accepted categories. They distorted what was considered "normal" or "beautiful." They messed with accepted patterns. They were, as they came to be called, "grotesque."

Many terms have been used to describe the grotesque. One list includes the following: "peculiar, odd, absurd, bizarre, macabre, depraved, degenerate, perverse."[15] These descriptions—and many others—all have their place in the rich history of the grotesque. But those original murals in the grotto continue to supply one central aspect that runs throughout understandings of the grotesque in its various forms. The grotesque—in art, literature, photography, architecture, life—embodies contradictions, incongruities. It engages in radical, at times shocking, *hybrid* forms that subvert dominant categories and resist resolution. The grotesque is composed, as someone put it, of "discombobulating juxtapositions" and bizarre combinations that "open up an indeterminate space of conflicting possibilities, images, and figures."[16] The grotesque trades in paradoxical anomalies that transgress binaries and cross classificatory boundaries. As a result, the grotesque usually involves *both* a subversion of the status quo *and*, in the words of Russian philosopher and literary critic Mikhail Bakhtin, "the potentiality of another world, another order, another way of life."[17]

As should be evident, the grotesque is inseparable from context. The murals in the grottos were certainly not viewed as grotesque when they were created. The figures in them probably didn't seem incongruous or contradictory at all; they simply represented a different symbolic or metaphorical system. But in the context of different aesthetic norms, they *became* grotesque. As Polish artist Ewa Kuryluk writes,

> The meaning of the grotesque is constituted by the norm which it contradicts: the order it destroys, the values it upsets, the authority and morality it derides, the religion it ridicules, the harmony

---

14. Kayser, *Grotesque*, 19–21; Adams and Yates, eds., *Grotesque in Art and Literature*, 6.
15. Edwards and Graulund, *Grotesque*, 1.
16. Edwards and Graulund, *Grotesque*, 3.
17. Mikhail Bakhtin, *Rabelais and His World*, trans. Helene Iswolsky (Bloomington: Indiana University Press, 1984), 230.

it breaks up, the heaven it brings down to earth, the position of classes, races, and sexes it reverses, the beauty and goodness it questions. The word "grotesque" makes sense only if one knows what the "norm" represents—in art and in life.[18]

Not surprisingly, any genre as subversive and unstable as the grotesque will generate a wide range of responses. For some, usually those who benefit from the norms, the grotesque is ominous and threatening; it inspires terror and fear. It opens the space for sinister invaders of the familiar world.[19] Consider some of Edgar Allan Poe's stories, many of which he called "Tales of the Grotesque." For others, usually those oppressed or excluded by the norms, the grotesque can be a liberating means of resistance; it can be something joyful and life-giving, something to celebrate.[20] More often than not, however, responses to the grotesque are themselves contradictory and incongruous; they include *both* repulsion *and* attraction, revulsion *and* fascination, horror *and* laughter, anxiety *and* liberation—all at the same time.

Much like the responses elicited by another ancient Roman work of art—the familiar *Alexamenos graffito* (ca. 238–244). It's a piece of Roman graffiti scratched in the plaster of a wall near the Palatine Hill in Rome. The image shows a figure with an ass's head and a human body hanging from a cross. In front of the figure stands a young man—presumably Alexamenos—raising his hand as if in prayer. Across the picture is written in broad strokes: *Alexamenos worships his God.*[21]

This graffiti takes Jesus down into the grotto. The image subverts normative categories; it joins elements that simply don't belong together: the divine, the human, the animal, all hanging together from a cross—a place where God is surely absent. Yet Alexamenos worships this figure as God. Not surprisingly, the graffiti mocks this impossible mixture of categories, revealing just how incongruous and contradictory these dizzying combinations really are. The

---

18. Kuryluk, *Salome and Judas*, 11.
19. See Kayser, *Grotesque*, e.g., 31–37.
20. See Bakhtin, *Rabelais*, where the grotesque is connected to the joyous and subversive celebration of carnival. Bakhtin's approach is examined more fully in chapter 3.
21. See Charles L. Campbell and Johan H. Cilliers, *Preaching Fools: The Gospel as a Rhetoric of Folly* (Waco, TX: Baylor University Press, 2012), 2–6.

divine–the human–the nonhuman hanging on a cross. It's repulsive and fascinating. It's disgusting and comical. It's scandalous—offensive. It's *grotesque*. But in a profound sense, it's *gospel*.

And therein lies the challenge for preaching—and for theology. The crucifixion is grotesque not simply because it is gruesome and horrifying (though it is). Rather, the crucifixion is grotesque because it is marked by irresolvable contradictions that the church has spent millennia tying itself in knots trying to form into a pattern. The Divine-Human One or the Human-Divine One hanging from a cross.[22] Crucified Messiah. Crucified Lord. Crucified God. These were incommensurable realities. The shocking incongruities exploded the dominant cultural categories; they subverted the familiar patterns of power and wisdom and divinity. We should speak of the perilous paradoxicality of the cross. It was a scandal—an offense. It was grotesque.

New Testament scholars have highlighted this character of crucifixion, even when they haven't used the term "grotesque." Alexandra Brown, for example, notes that Paul in First Corinthians preaches a scandalous gospel with unconventional, "destabilizing pairings of opposites."[23] He seeks to "perceptually unbalance" the church.[24] Weak power, foolish wisdom. Crucified Messiah. Crucified Lord. Paul cannot preach with nice, neat patterns because he's trying to proclaim a grotesque gospel, which resists normative rhetorical categories.

Paul is actually a homiletics professor's nightmare (and not just because he needs serious work on issues of gender, sexuality, and slavery). What are you going to say in a sermon conference with the apostle? "Paul, I think you need a little more clarity here. Let's see if you can come up with a good, sharp focus statement. You can't preach such an unsettling, contradictory Word. You're throwing the congregation off balance. After all, look at how the Corinthians are responding. They think you're nuts!" What the homiletics professor is really saying is something like this: "You need to back off the grotesque gospel, Paul. You need to arrive at some *resolution*. A clear

---

22. In chapters 2 and 4 I discuss the nonhuman, which is usually ignored.
23. Alexandra R. Brown, *The Cross and Human Transformation: Paul's Apocalyptic Word in 1 Corinthians* (Minneapolis: Fortress Press, 1995), 30.
24. Brown, *Cross and Human Transformation*, 158.

doctrine of the atonement would be helpful. Such 'discombobulating juxtapositions' just won't preach."

Roy Harrisville, another New Testament scholar, counters the homiletics professor with a jarring point: the cross, he says, "fractures" all of our rhetoric and theology. Paul, he writes, "could not master his theology in any ultimate way because it never existed as a system; in fact, it could not, since the event at its core [crucifixion] spelled the *death of system*."[25] Or, we might say, the death of pattern. And Harrisville makes the same argument for *all* of the New Testament authors. As Richard Lischer put it concisely in his critique of narrative preaching: "The cross is a catastrophe that interrupts all of our neat and settled narratives."[26]

The responses to crucifixion also have the incongruous, paradoxical character of the grotesque. Terror and horror and revulsion are obvious—aspects that an emphasis on folly alone does not take seriously enough. But these responses merge with curiosity and fascination and even blood-thirst. Crucifixions drew a crowd.

In the face of the grotesque cross, another response is shocking: laughter. Yes, laughter. We see it in the mocking of Jesus present in the Gospel accounts themselves. There were actually many crucifixion jokes, as well as comedies depicting Christ's passion.[27] Indeed, the *Alexamenos graffito* was itself a kind of crucifixion joke. Monty Python's *Life of Brian* did not originate laughter at the cross.

But this laughter took various forms. For those in power the cross generated a kind of mocking laughter that reinforced the horrific instrument of execution through which the elites maintained their dominance. For the "low and despised," however, those threatened by crucifixion, there was a kind of gallows humor that may have helped to blunt the horror of the punishment.[28]

---

25. Roy A. Harrisville, *Fracture: The Cross as Irreconcilable in the Language and Thought of the Biblical Writers* (Grand Rapids: Eerdmans, 2006), 108. Italics added.

26. Richard Lischer, "The Limits of Story," *Interpretation* 38 (January 1984): 33.

27. On crucifixion jokes, see Justin Meggit, "Laughing and Dreaming at the Foot of the Cross: Context and Reception of a Religious Symbol?" in *Modern Spiritualities: An Inquiry*, ed. Laurence Brown, Bernard C. Farr, and R. Joseph Hoffmann (Amherst, MA: Prometheus Books, 1997), 63–70. For an example of a comic passion play, see Michael O'Connell, "Mockery, Farce, and *Risus Paschalis* in the York *Christ before Herod*," in *Farce and Farcical Elements*, ed. Wim Husken, Ludus: Medieval and Early Renaissance Theatre and Drama 6 (Amsterdam: Rodopi, 2002), 45–58.

28. L. L. Welborn, *Paul, the Fool of Christ: A Study of 1 Corinthians 1–4 in the Comic-Philosophic Tradition* (London: T & T Clark, 2005), 101.

But at the deepest level there was what I would now call *grotesque laughter*. Such laughter expresses the disruptive, inexpressible incongruities at the heart of the gospel. God-cross. Life-death. Repulsion-fascination. Horror-hope. It is laughter that recognizes the impossibility of ever capturing or controlling the cross in human categories or systems or doctrines. It is the kind of laughter that, in the words of D. Diane Davis, "breaks up" our totalities, our patterns, our norms.[29] As theologian Jacqueline Bussie writes, such "laughter functions as an apposite extra-linguistic resource for expression of a theology of the cross because a theology of the cross is inherently paradoxical, resistant to linguistic expressibility, and resultant from a collision of narratives."[30] It is laughter in response to a gospel that remains "scandalous and inscrutable."[31] It is laughter in the face of the grotesque.

Destabilizing pairings of opposites. Fractured categories and norms. Horror, revulsion, fascination, laughter. Crucifixion takes us into what historian Geoffrey Harpham has called the "interval" of the grotesque. In the interval of the grotesque, he argues, we recognize a number of different forms in an object. But we have not yet developed a clear sense of how those elements are organized into a whole.[32] The object remains "just out of focus, just beyond the reach of language."[33] In this interval, as Harpham puts it, "The mind is poised between death and rebirth, insanity and discovery, rubble and revelation."[34]

That's the interval created by the gospel. It is the interval in which we now live as Christians—"between death and rebirth, insanity and discovery, rubble and revelation." It is the interval in which the preacher lives. There is no avoiding it. For the event in which Christ identifies most deeply with humanity is a grotesque event of unresolved contradictions and incongruities; it embodies the perilous paradoxicality of human life; it cannot be forced into a nice, neat pattern.

---

29. D. Diane Davis, *Breaking Up [at] Totality: A Rhetoric of Laughter* (Carbondale: Southern Illinois University Press, 2000).

30. Jacqueline Bussie, *The Laughter of the Oppressed: Ethical and Theological Resistance in Wiesel, Morrison, and Endo* (New York: T & T Clark, 2007), 122.

31. Bussie, *Laughter of the Oppressed*, 120.

32. Geoffrey Galt Harpham, *On the Grotesque: Strategies of Contradiction in Art and Literature* (Princeton, NJ: Princeton University Press, 1982), 16.

33. Harpham, *On the Grotesque*, 3.

34. Harpham, *On the Grotesque*, 18.

As a consequence, the Christian life itself is a *hybrid* life—a both-and life—a life in the interval in which the central event of redemption is simultaneously a horrific event of violence and suffering—an event in which God is both scandalous and inscrutable. And that is what makes the Christian life grotesque. It is not just that the evil in the world, lifted up in the crucifixion, is so horrific, though it is. It is that as Christians we live in this deep, unresolved incongruity. The new creation, we proclaim, has interrupted the old age. But everywhere we look we see crucified masses of human beings, suffering beyond what many of us can even comprehend. And now in the face of climate change, all of humanity lives in the shadow of death. We live, as Kenneth Surin notes, simultaneously with a testimony of faithful affirmation *and* a testimony of that faith's negation.[35] And Jesus embodies all of those contradictions on his grotesque cross.

Preaching a Grotesque Gospel

A grotesque gospel presents a challenge for theology and preaching. Many of us don't want to live with the scandalous and inscrutable—even though we know that reality all too well. As a result, many of us try to force the gospel into our doctrines of the atonement, our theological systems, and our homiletical theories; we seek to get control of the contradictions. As Willie Jennings has described "academic theology," it "flows from an intellectual posture created through the cultivated capacities to clarify, categorize, define, explain." This posture, he notes, eclipses theology's "fluid, adaptable, even morph-able character."[36] But the grotesque gospel calls precisely for this fluid, adaptable, morph-able theology.

Like the theologians Jennings describes, too many preachers, myself included, likewise rush too quickly to escape the interval of the grotesque. That's our purpose, isn't it? Surely our goal is clarity, security, certainty. Give people a nice, focused nugget to carry

---

35. Kenneth Surin, "Taking Suffering Seriously," in *The Problem of Evil: Selected Readings*, ed. Michael Peterson (Notre Dame: Notre Dame University Press, 1992), 344; cited in Bussie, *Laughter of the Oppressed*, 46.
36. Willie James Jennings, *The Christian Imagination: Theology and the Origins of Race* (New Haven, CT: Yale University Press, 2010), 8.

home—not the shocking, unresolved contradictions of a grotesque gospel. We preachers often seem to have a "rage for order," but, unlike the line in Wallace Stevens's poem, I'm not so sure it's *blessed*.[37] For when we rush to order, when we avoid the interval of the grotesque, our preaching may become shallow, unreal, clichéd. We don't go deep enough. We're not honest enough. And we end up falsifying both the gospel and life itself—we end up imposing false patterns. The grotesque gospel, however, calls preachers to relinquish our familiar patterns.

In his historical novel *Silence*, Shusaku Endo depicts a descent—or is it an *a*scent?—into a grotesque gospel.[38] The novel takes place in seventeenth-century Japan, a time when Christians were undergoing extreme persecution. Father Sebastian Rodrigues travels from Portugal to Japan as a Jesuit missionary. He's following his mentor, Father Fierrarra, who has himself, to the horror of his students, apparently committed apostasy.

Rodrigues begins his mission as an underground priest with a grand and beautiful ideal both of Christ and of the missionary. He looks down on those who would deny their faith and apostatize. As Jacqueline Bussie notes, Rodrigues starts out with clear, either-or, binary patterns: a person is strong or weak, honored or shamed, righteous or sinner, courageous or fearful, saved or condemned—ultimately either a believer or an apostate.[39] Along the way, however, as he witnesses the torture of Christian peasants and faces the terror of torture himself, Rodrigues enters into a grotesque gospel. His neat categories fall apart. His binaries no longer work. Nothing is as clear as he had thought. The martyrdoms he witnesses are not glorious, but horrifying and humiliating. Courage and strength alone do not define discipleship. Righteousness and sinfulness are not so easily distinguished. As his neat binaries collapse, Rodrigues wonders, "Why is human life so full of grotesque irony?"[40]

Finally, having been captured, Rodrigues is taken to the pit and brought before the fumie—the crucifix on which one steps to commit

---

37. Wallace Stevens, "The Idea of Order at Key West," in *The Collected Poems of Wallace Stevens* (New York: Alfred A. Knopf, 1976), 128–30.

38. Shusaku Endo, *Silence*, trans. William Johnston (New York: Taplinger, 1980).

39. My interpretation of Endo's novel follows that of Bussie, *Laughter of the Oppressed*, 77–124. Bussie does not interpret the gospel as grotesque.

40. Endo, *Silence*, 162.

apostasy. As he stands above the fumie, he can hear the screams of others being tortured. And his captors tell him that if he steps on the fumie, if he commits apostasy, their torture will end, their suffering will cease. It's a lie, of course. But that is what he is told. As he looks at Jesus' face on the fumie, he no longer sees the beautiful face he has imagined, but an ugly, suffering face, worn down and concave from all the feet that have stepped on it. And finally Jesus breaks his silence and speaks to Rodrigues for the first time: "Trample! Trample!" he says. "I more than anyone know of the pain in your foot. It was to be trampled on by men that I was born into this world. It was to share men's pain that I carried my cross."[41] And Rodrigues steps on the fumie.

Confronted with the suffering of the world and the incongruities of the cross, Rodrigues has to give up his old categories, his old patterns, including his understanding of weak and strong, faith and apostasy; he even gives up his vocation. He has apostatized, but he nevertheless affirms that his faith remains. There's an unresolved resolution to the narrative. Rodrigues enters into the perilous paradoxicality of life—and faith. At the moment of his apostasy he may have actually been his most Christ-like, giving himself for the sake of others. Or is he simply justifying his apostasy, as some people claim? Rodrigues enters the interval between a testimony of faithful affirmation and a testimony of that faith's negation. He becomes, in Bussie's phrase, a "believing apostate,"[42] forever to live his life "poised between death and rebirth, insanity and discovery, rubble and revelation." Faced with this scandalous and inscrutable gospel, Rodrigues makes a telling comment about preaching: "I know that my Lord is different from the God that is preached in the churches."[43]

It is important to hear how Endo himself came to his theological insight: he *listened*. Here is what he said: "If [the Christians of that era] were to be divided into the weak and the strong, I would be among the former. . . . History knows their sufferings: I believed it was the task of the novelist to listen to their sufferings."[44] Endo didn't

---

41. Endo, *Silence*, 259.
42. Bussie, *Laughter of the Oppressed*, 77. Bussie also traces the role that laughter plays in the novel. It is the extralinguistic, grotesque laughter I discussed earlier in this chapter.
43. Endo, *Silence*, 264.
44. Quoted in Bussie, *Laughter of the Oppressed*, 79.

14   The Scandal of the Gospel

rush to impose his patterns on the apostates. He himself entered into the grotesque gospel. And I believe that's the appropriate stance for preachers as well. We also enter into the grotesque gospel by giving up our familiar patterns and our narrative resolutions—in order to listen. We enter the grotesque gospel by caring more for people than for patterns. Maybe that's the preacher's *kenosis*, the preacher's participation in crucifixion.

Sometimes we have to be shocked by the grotesque gospel in order to start listening. Several years ago I was on the campus of the University of Central America in San Salvador, El Salvador. At the center of that campus is a chapel—some people call it the chapel of the martyrs. It sits next to the site where in 1989 six Jesuit priests, their housekeeper, and her daughter were brutally murdered by commandos of the Salvadoran armed forces. The priests were working for peace in the land and justice for the poor—so they were slaughtered. Next to the chapel there is a memorial museum that tells the story of the martyrs, as well as others who were murdered. A copy of Jürgen Moltmann's book *The Crucified God*, in Spanish, is in the museum. It is stained with blood. It had apparently been knocked off a bookshelf when the martyrs were killed, and it had fallen into a pool of their blood.

When you walk into the chapel you face the chancel, with a series of panels on the wall. Even though the panels show scenes of the civil war in El Salvador, including mass graves and Óscar Romero's martyrdom, the images are bright and colorful. At the center is a large, beautiful cross, painted in celebratory hues. Beside the cross are paintings depicting what appeared to me to be the coming of the Holy Spirit and the resurrection or ascension or transfiguration.[45] Beside those images are two large, colorful angels. The "symmetry of the figures and the brightness of the colors illustrate the power of the Resurrection to bring order and beauty to the darkest places."[46] That's what you see as you face the front—as you are listening to the sermon.

But when you stand in the pulpit and you face the back of the

---

45. Edgardo Colón-Emeric has recently argued that transfiguration is a central theological emphasis in El Salvador. See *Óscar Romero's Theological Vision: Liberation and the Transfiguration of the Poor* (South Bend, IN: University of Notre Dame, 2018).
46. Colón-Emeric, *Óscar Romero's Theological Vision*, 169.

chapel, you see something very different. All across the back wall are depictions of the stations of the cross. They are large, graphic, black-and-white drawings of tortured human beings. Naked, disfigured bodies. Contorted faces. Gaping mouths. It was shocking to see such figures in a church. I was reminded how such images have almost become taboo in our sanctuaries, even though for centuries churches regularly depicted horrific scenes of demonic activity on sanctuary walls.

The pulpit in that chapel in San Salvador sits in a space of unresolved contradictions. One preaches there standing between the beautiful, colorful cross and the graphic, black-and-white images of torture. One preaches "poised between death and rebirth, insanity and discovery, rubble and revelation." And in that space none of my neat, familiar patterns would do.

I wonder now if many people aren't aching for this grotesque gospel—for preaching that moves beyond predictable patterns into the perilous, paradoxical depths of life. I wonder if faithful preaching of a grotesque gospel requires not clarifications and resolutions, but rather careful *descriptions* of our complex and unresolved human lives, into which we believe God has entered, even if those descriptions disturb our familiar homiletical patterns. Indeed, those descriptions may often be more redemptive than our imposed theological patterns.[47]

Not long ago I was leading a class discussion of Claudia Rankine's collection of poems *Citizen: An American Lyric*.[48] Over and over again the poems describe the dehumanizing realities of racism, particularly the microaggressions or everyday violence African American people endure. Throughout the book Rankine uses the second person—you, you, you—so the reader has to identify with these experiences. In introducing the book I said to the class, "This is a very difficult and painful book to read," which it was for *me*. Later, however, my teaching assistant was talking to a biracial woman, who was not in the class. The woman had read the book, and *she* commented, "It wasn't difficult for me to read at all. It was affirming. It confirmed a lifetime of experiences that I've had." Redemptive description. Maybe that is the place to begin.

---

47. For a discussion of the importance of description in preaching, see Anna Carter Florence, *Preaching as Testimony* (Louisville, KY: Westminster John Knox Press, 2007), 143–50.
48. Claudia Rankine, *Citizen: An American Lyric* (Minneapolis: Graywolf Press, 2014).

Anna Akhmatova was a beloved Russian poet who suffered greatly along with countless others through two world wars, the Russian Revolution, and especially the Stalinist terror. Her husband was executed and her son was imprisoned for many years. She herself was persecuted, condemned by the Central Committee to a civic death. Her poems had to be kept alive by people who memorized them. Someone once described her with words that were spoken about Dante: "That's the one who was in hell."[49] Her extraordinary poem-cycle, *Requiem*, which deals with the time of the terror, contains haunting echoes of the crucifixion.

Years ago my former colleague Anna Carter Florence introduced me to the short poem that opens *Requiem*. The poem is titled "Instead of a Preface." It takes place as Akhmatova stands in line with other women waiting for news of their loved ones, who have been imprisoned during the repression run by Nikolai Yezhov, a Soviet secret-police official. She writes,

> In the terrible years of the Yezhov terror, I spent seventeen months in the prison lines of Leningrad. Once, someone "recognized" me. Then a woman with bluish lips standing behind me, who, of course, had never heard me called by name before, woke up from the stupor to which everyone had succumbed and whispered in my ear (everyone spoke in whispers there):
> "Can you describe this?"
> And I answered: "Yes, I can."
> Then something that looked like a smile passed over what had once been her face.[50]

Maybe that is the place to begin.

---

49. *A Film about Anna Akhmatova* (New York: Das Films, TurnstyleTV, 2008).
50. Anna Akhmatova, *Requiem*, in *The Complete Poems of Anna Akhmatova*, trans. Judith Hemschemeyer, ed. Roberta Reeder (Somerville, MA: Zephyr Press, 1990), 95.

Chapter 2

The Thing

Resisting the Weaponized Grotesque

As I noted in chapter 1, Edgar Allan Poe wrote many "tales of the grotesque," as he even titled some of them.¹ His well-known grotesque stories, like "The Fall of the House of Usher" and "The Masque of the Red Death," are unsettlingly mysterious; they are ominous and threatening, often inspiring a visceral terror. Poe was a master of this particular kind of grotesque tale. Poe, however, is also considered to be the inventor of the modern detective story, beginning with his groundbreaking work in the genre, "The Murders in the Rue Morgue."² These stories Poe called "tales of ratiocination."³ In them the detective uses uncanny reason and analysis to solve a mystery and restore order. It is as if the tales of ratiocination are the polar opposite of the tales of the grotesque.

In "The Murders in the Rue Morgue," however, the detective story actually employs the grotesque—though in a distinctive and deeply disturbing way. I will spare you most of the gory details. Suffice it to say that a mother and daughter are brutally murdered late at night in their fourth-floor bedroom. As Poe's amateur detective, Auguste Dupin, states, the murders involved "an agility astounding, a strength superhuman, a ferocity brutal, a butchery without motive,

---

1. His first collection of stories, published in 1840, was titled *Tales of the Grotesque and Arabesque.*
2. The other two important stories are "The Purloined Letter" and "The Mystery of Marie Roget." See Edgar Allan Poe, *The Detective Stories of Edgar Allan Poe* (Los Angeles: Sugar Skull Press, 2015).
3. On Poe's tales of the grotesque and tales of ratiocination, see Wilbur S. Scott, "Introduction," in *Edgar Allan Poe: Complete Tales and Poems* (Edison, NJ: Castle Books, 2002), ix–xi.

a *grotesquerie* in horror absolutely alien from humanity."⁴ Moreover, the facts of the case lead nowhere. There appears to be no way a murderer could have gained access to the room where the murders took place. There's no apparent way the person could have escaped. There's no way anyone would have had the strength to do what was done.

To make a long story short, following pages of "ratiocination," Dupin concludes that it was not a human who committed the murders. It was an orangutan, who had been brought to the city from Borneo by a sailor. The orangutan had escaped, climbed up the side of the building and through a window, committed the grotesque murders, and left by the same route. The murder is solved, the orangutan is captured, and order is restored.

If only it were that simple. But it's not. Poe's story confronts us with an exceedingly ugly side of the grotesque. And we cannot avoid this ugly side. In our current context, we need to name some things.

Poe's story was written in 1841 in Philadelphia, where Poe had lived since late 1837 or early 1838.⁵ The abolitionist movement was growing, and racial tensions in the city were high. There was anxiety among whites about the intermixing of the races. In addition, there was concern over the growth of Black wealth and status in Philadelphia. For the antiabolitionists, Black people were becoming arrogant and challenging the social hierarchy. Sexual and economic anxieties merged to create volatile racial conflict during the six years Poe was in Philadelphia. In 1838, for example, one of the largest antiabolitionist riots occurred in the city. Pennsylvania Hall had been built by abolitionists as a center where people of different races gathered for free discussion. But the grand building was depicted by antiabolitionists as a place of unbridled extramarital passions between Black

---

4. Edgar Allan Poe, "The Murders in the Rue Morgue," in *Detective Stories*, 42.
5. My treatment of "The Murders in the Rue Morgue" draws on several sources: Leonard Cassuto, *The Inhuman Race: The Racial Grotesque in American Literature and Culture* (New York: Columbia University Press, 1997), 160–61; Elise Lemire, "Combating Abolitionism with the Species Argument: Race and Economic Anxieties in Poe's Philadelphia," in *"Miscegenation": Making Race in America* (Philadelphia: University of Pennsylvania Press, 2002), 87–114; Jessica Metzler, "Lusty Ape-Men and Imperiled White Womanhood: Reading Race in a 1930s Poe Film Adaptation," in *Adapting Poe: Re-Imaginings in Popular Culture*, ed. Carl H. Sederholm (New York: Palgrave Macmillan, 2012), 31–43; and Christopher Peterson, "The Aping Apes of Poe and Wright: Race, Animality, and Mimicry in 'The Murders in the Rue Morgue' and *Native Son*," *New Literary History* 41 (2010): 151–71.

men and white women. So in May 1838 a mob burned the building to the ground as the authorities looked the other way. This kind of racial tension is the context of Poe's story.

Numerous scholars agree that "The Murders in the Rue Morgue" is a coded story in which the threat of the criminal Black man—particularly his threat to white women—is depicted in the figure of the orangutan. Poe was drawing on popular caricatures of the time that depicted Black men as primates, as well as on popular myths that orangutans in particular desired human women.[6] According to some, Poe was actually inspired by separate Philadelphia newspaper accounts of a Negro murderer and an escaped orangutan.[7] So, in the words of literary scholar Leonard Cassuto, "[Poe] conflates the two into a darkly colored ape who viciously kills white women." The Black man becomes literally nonhuman. And the story creates "a mood verging on panic in which all black men are suspect."[8]

Here the restoration of order involves the capture and control of the inhuman one—the animal, the ape—who threatens the white order of things. Poe's move is significant. He both criminalizes and dehumanizes the Black man, a racist configuration of labels that has driven the treatment of African American men from the post-slavery era of convict leasing to the current system of mass incarceration.[9] This dehumanizing act is the consequence of fear and anxiety on the part of those in power. It is the result of changing times when the white population sees its status threatened and seeks to assert what it views as the "normal" order of things, the "normal" hierarchy of being.[10]

6. Lemire, *"Miscegenation,"* 100.
7. Cassuto, *Inhuman Race*, 160.
8. Cassuto, *Inhuman Race*, 160.
9. On convict leasing, see Douglas Blackmon, *Slavery by Another Name: The Re-Enslavement of Black Americans from the Civil War to World War II* (New York: Anchor, 2008). During the period of convict leasing that followed slavery in the United States, Black people were imprisoned on trumped-up charges. They were then leased out to companies as interchangeable, disposable tools in the service of industry. They were literally worked to death. On the emergence of mass incarceration from the history of slavery and convict leasing, see Michelle Alexander, *The New Jim Crow: Mass Incarceration in the Age of Colorblindness* (New York: New Press, 2010).
10. John Scaggs argues that crime fiction has often functioned to reaffirm and restore the dominant social order. See John Scaggs, *Crime Fiction*, New Critical Idiom (London: Routledge, 2005), 45–46. More recently, John Fram has demonstrated that white crime writers have often justified police brutality. He quotes novelist Steph Cha, who states that the "return

As I noted in chapter 1, popular crime fiction does many different things. What Poe's story does, I want to suggest, is *weaponize* the grotesque. The grotesque becomes a "powerful ideological weapon."[11] The grotesque, as I have argued, involves mixing categories—in the grotto it even involved mixing human and animal categories. But while the grotesque is theologically and homiletically disruptive in valuable ways, it can also be used as a dehumanizing weapon. Those in power can employ the grotesque to denigrate people who are different from them in order to reassert their power and reinforce social hierarchies. They can use the grotesque to scapegoat groups, projecting their own frustrations onto them and blaming them for the problems in the larger society. Using language that turns humans into *animals* is one way of doing this. Using language that turns them into *things* is another. Using caricature—the freakish exaggeration of certain body parts—is yet another. And this use of the grotesque often occurs during times of transition when change feels threatening to some, and fear and anxiety are prevalent. In particular, the weaponized grotesque—or what Cassuto calls the "racial grotesque"—has appeared when ideologically constructed whiteness and white supremacy feel threatened.

Poe's story is thus not just a literary curiosity. The weaponized grotesque has been employed throughout history against countless groups in addition to African Americans: Native Americans, Japanese Americans during World War II, Jewish people, immigrants, LGBTQ+ people, disabled people. Even Barack and Michelle Obama were depicted as monkeys. And think of the charge of "bestiality" leveled at LGBTQ+ persons. Or a radio host calling protestors at the Kavanaugh Supreme Court hearing "screaming animals." Or Donald Trump calling women pigs and a Black woman a "lowlife dog." Or Eric Trump referring to Black Lives Matter protestors as "animals." And, of course, there's the former president's language for immigrants: They're "animals." They're "aliens." They're "infesting" our country like vermin. So their children are put in

---

to order from chaos" in crime fiction "requires an assumption that the justice system resolving this chaos is a functioning system, which, clearly, it isn't." See John Fram, "How White Crime Writers Justified Police Brutality," *New York Times*, June 4, 2020. In this sense, some crime fiction, though certainly not all, may implicitly continue the trajectory of Poe's initial work.

11. Lemire, *"Miscegenation,"* 111.

cages. Social psychologists even have a term for this: "animalistic dehumanization."[12]

In addition, people get turned into *things*. The former president tweets about a "flood" or infestation of immigrants; human beings become a natural disaster. Churches turn LGBTQ+ persons into *issues* to be debated. In the news we are regularly reminded of the ways women are treated as things—objects. Women still have to claim, "We are people too!"[13] People in prison are reduced to numbers—they become *things* so those on the outside need not engage their humanity. The practice continues today in for-profit prisons, where human beings become commodities, sources of profit on an accountant's ledger.[14]

And, of course, *things* don't have *feelings*. They don't have human emotions. So immigrant families seeking asylum can be separated from each other; children can be torn from their parents without a twinge of conscience—and without a plan for reuniting them. The same was assumed of slaves, who also endured repeated family separations. And people in prison are also separated from their families, not only by bars and Plexiglas, but also by great distances.

The dehumanizing, weaponized grotesque—used to create fear, anger, and disgust at the targeted group—is one of the most important rhetorical tools for maintaining a threatened white, male, heterosexual—and even Christian—order. Amid our shifting cultural landscape, much political rhetoric today is shaped by an explicit *reassertion* of the weaponized grotesque. The rhetoric has always been there, but it has often been more coded, more deniable. But in recent years the grotesque has been openly reasserted. And as social psychologists are demonstrating, this use of dehumanizing political rhetoric can be effective. It can shape attitudes toward the targeted groups.[15]

---

12. See Stephen M. Utych, "How Dehumanization Influences Attitudes toward Immigrants," *Political Research Quarterly* 71, no. 2 (2018): 440–52.
13. Betty Friedan, "Women Are People Too," *Good Housekeeping*, September 1960.
14. See Andrew Krinks, "Why It Pays to Imprison: Unmasking the Prison-Industrial Complex," in *And the Criminals with Him: Essays in Honor of Will D. Campbell and All the Reconciled*, ed. Will D. Campbell and Richard C. Goode (Eugene, OR: Cascade, 2012), 54–69.
15. Utych, "How Dehumanization Influences Attitudes toward Immigrants."

Resisting the Weaponized Grotesque

Demetria Martinez is a poet, novelist, and social activist. For many years she has been an advocate for refugees and immigrants. In one of her poems, "Upon Waking," Martinez depicts the inevitable consequences of the weaponized grotesque—and she points to a response.

> *for Amadou Diallo, shot 41 times by police officers*
> *as he reached for his wallet, New York City, 1999*
> In a dream after your death I stood on the rocky
> Shores of an island. Dark-skinned people, young
> And old, pressed against boulders as helicopter
> Gunships took aim. I cried out at a wall of wind:
> "No, stop, they have histories!"—but it was too late.
> The soldiers were acting in self-defense
> Against the sudden move;
> A people firing a round
> Of stories that might
> Have opened hearts
> Locked down as the
> Lids of caskets.[16]

As Martinez reveals, the consequence of the weaponized grotesque is death. Literal death. Once people become things or animals, their lives don't matter. They can be killed, mowed down without a second thought. They can be suffocated, shot point-blank, shot in the back as they run away—and there will often be no charges, no convictions. But simultaneously, Martinez suggests, there is death among those who weaponize the grotesque, those who do the killing. It is what some have called the "death of the moral conscience"[17] or the "death of the moral imagination."[18] Their hearts are "locked down as the lids of caskets."

In the midst of this chaotic, destructive swirl of death, Martinez calls preachers to the necessary response: "No, stop!" Preachers are

---

16. Demetria Martinez, "Upon Waking," in *The Devil's Workshop* (Tucson: University of Arizona Press, 2002), 31.
17. William Stringfellow, *An Ethic for Christians and Other Aliens in a Strange Land* (1973; reprint, Eugene, OR: Wipf and Stock, 2004), 106.
18. Sharon D. Welch, *A Feminist Ethic of Risk*, rev. ed. (Minneapolis: Fortress Press, 2000), 11.

called to interrupt the weaponized grotesque that leads to death. "No, stop!" These people are not animals. They are not aliens. They are not issues. They are not infesting our country. They do not belong in cages. "No, stop!" Then Martinez goes a step further, suggesting a direction for resistance. "No, stop, they have histories"—they have "stories that might [open] hearts." Listen! The first step of resistance is to declare, "No, stop!" to the weaponized grotesque. Then we attend to the histories and stories that unmask dehumanizing systems and reveal the humanity of those who have been turned into animals or things.

This humanizing is always possible because, as I've noted, the grotesque is always unstable. The weaponzied grotesque can never fully stick because the combined categories of human-animal or human-thing are incongruous; they are unsettled. Indeed, the grotesque itself subverts the very attempts to use it to objectify or animalize another human being. The humanity of the victims can never be erased; it is always present, always reasserting itself. As Cassuto reminds us, the grotesque by definition is liminal, in-between, unsettled; it cannot be hardened into stone. And that, Cassuto suggests, is a source of hope. As he writes,

> The grotesque is a threat to the system of knowledge by virtue of its liminal position within the system. This liminality demands resolution; for a human being caught between the categories of human and thing, the pressure will be exerted toward a return to the human category, for that is the only choice that offers the possibility of resolution.[19]

It is thus no wonder that the efforts to dehumanize often grow more and more intense as the humanity of others reasserts itself. It takes more effort to maintain the weaponized grotesque. But it is precisely into this unstable situation that preachers are called to speak a counter-rhetoric. And this rhetoric often takes the form of counter-stories, counter-histories that resist and subvert the false patterns of the weaponized grotesque.

We hear this refrain from oppressed groups throughout history— the refrain of reclaiming their humanity. The question attributed to

---

19. Cassuto, *Inhuman Race*, xvii.

24   The Scandal of the Gospel

Sojourner Truth, "Ain't I a Woman?" echoes through the generations. And from Frederick Douglass to the sanitation workers in Memphis, the refrain sounds: "I AM A MAN." And some people listen, and the caskets of their hearts creak open, even if just a bit. So it goes, with groups struggling to resist the weaponized grotesque and reclaim their humanity. Preachers are called to join the resistance.

In 1852, about a decade after Poe's detective story, another important work of popular fiction was published. It was a counter-story to Poe's. It was really a sermon, combining biblical texts and story and direct address to the reader. Indeed, it is simultaneously one of the most effective and *controversial* sermons in U.S. history. The novel was addressed to the dominant, white majority—to those responsible for dehumanizing others. And it sought to counter the weaponized grotesque that undergirded the system of slavery. I'm referring to Harriet Beecher Stowe's novel *Uncle Tom's Cabin*.[20]

The novel, as everyone recognizes, is troubling; it is filled with incongruities. On the one hand, in Stowe's ugly context the book was audacious and scandalous. It was a powerful piece of protest fiction, written out of Stowe's outrage over the Fugitive Slave Act.[21] It was a bold and courageous word, much more daring than most of the sermons I have preached. On the other hand, the novel is profoundly disturbing. At times it is patronizing—or better matronizing—toward Black people. At points it infantilizes African Americans. It contains generalizations about race that are outlandish and racist. And there are good reasons why "Uncle Tom" became a dismissive epithet for a passive, servile Black person.[22] It is a troubling book addressed to a horrific situation.[23]

---

20. Harriet Beecher Stowe, *Uncle Tom's Cabin* (Mineola, NY: Dover Publications, Dover Thrift Editions, 2005).
21. Joan D. Hedrick, *Harriet Beecher Stowe: A Life* (New York: Oxford University Press, 1994), 202.
22. As Joan Hedrick notes, Stowe's position, which she later moved beyond, has been labeled "'romantic racialism,' a blend of philanthropic and paternalistic attitudes toward blacks," in which African Americans are essentially different from whites and especially open to the "sweeter graces of the Christian religion." Romantic racialism was widespread by 1851. Hedrick, *Harriet Beecher Stowe*, 209–10; see also Robert S. Levine, "Introduction," in Harriet Beecher Stowe, *Dred: A Tale of the Great Dismal Swamp* (1856; reprint, New York: Penguin, 2000), xii, xvi.
23. It is important to note that *Uncle Tom's Cabin* is not Stowe's only or final response to race and slavery in the United States. She listened to criticisms, and her position continued

Controversial as it is, homileticians nevertheless need to attend to the novel for a couple of reasons. First, along with other works of sentimental fiction, it is significant in the history of preaching. Moreover, it is critically important for recognizing and reclaiming the historical role of *women* preachers. This fact creates an inescapable tension in dealing with the novel. One needs to value its role in the history of preaching without excusing its problematic racial dynamics. Homileticians need to examine both the contributions and problems of the novel, but we really haven't yet in any detail.[24] Second, the novel is worth examining because Stowe seeks directly to resist the weaponized grotesque. That is the purpose of her sermon. Preachers can learn both from her resistance and, importantly, from her *limitations*.

Preachers of the Fictional Page

Through her novels, Harriet Beecher Stowe, along with other popular women novelists of the nineteenth century, influenced the preaching of her day and the field of homiletics, although that influence has been largely ignored in our discipline. In some ways Stowe indirectly

---

to evolve and change, though even her later ideas would remain problematic today: "There is considerable evidence . . . that Stowe remained not only highly responsive to debates on slavery and race after the publication of *Uncle Tom's Cabin*, but also surprisingly willing to rethink, modify, and revise her views." Her later novel, *Dred*, for example, though containing conflicting perspectives, "can be read as Stowe's thoughtful novelistic response to the changing political and cultural climate of the mid-1850s, and as her own highly mediated 'response' to *Uncle Tom's Cabin*." In the novel, which has a violent Black revolutionary, the fictional son of Denmark Vesey, as its central character, Stowe "revises her racialist representations, attempts new strategies of point of view that would allow for a fuller development of black revolutionary perspectives, and implicitly rejects African colonizationism—endorsed in *Uncle Tom's Cabin*—as a solution to the nation's racial problems." Stowe even presents "violent rebellion as a logical, perhaps even sacred response to slavery" (Levine, "Introduction," x, xxx).

24. For a couple of articles that briefly examine the novel homiletically, see David S. Reynolds, "From Doctrine to Narrative: The Rise of Pulpit Storytelling in America," *American Quarterly* 32, no. 5 (Winter 1980): 479–98; and Charles L. Campbell, "A Not-So-Distant Mirror: Nineteenth-Century Popular Fiction and Pulpit Storytelling," *Theology Today* 51 (January 1995): 574–82. For a broader look at Stowe's novels in the context of religious literature in the United States, see David S. Reynolds, *Faith in Fiction: The Emergence of Religious Literature in America* (Cambridge, MA: Harvard University Press, 1981).

shaped preaching as much as her father, Lyman, and brother, Henry. She deserves some time in a Beecher Lecture.

Unable to preach from pulpits themselves, popular women novelists became what historian Mary Kelley calls "preachers of the fictional page."[25] Indeed, Stowe herself wrote, "It is as much my vocation to preach on paper as it is that of my brothers to preach viva voce."[26] In this vein Ann Douglas said of *Uncle Tom's Cabin* itself: It "is a great book, not because it is a great novel, but because it is a great revival sermon, aimed directly at the conversion of its hearers."[27] Others have noted that the novel provides a classic example of the jeremiad—a familiar form of political sermon inspired by the exhortations of the Old Testament prophets.[28] Indeed, Jane Tompkins has argued that "Stowe's novel provides the most obvious and compelling instance of the jeremiad since the Great Awakening."[29] Through *Uncle Tom's Cabin*, Stowe was preaching.

Like Stowe, other popular women novelists preached through their fictional pages. They also did some homiletics. They critiqued, sometimes hilariously, the abstract preaching of their day that was divorced from the realities of life. Stowe herself wrote of Samuel Hopkins in her novel *The Minister's Wooing*, "The only mistake made by the good man was that of supposing that the elaboration of theology was preaching the gospel."[30] In place of this abstract, doc-

---

25. Mary Kelley, *Private Woman, Public Stage: Literary Domesticity in Nineteenth-Century America* (1984; reprint, Chapel Hill: University of North Carolina Press, 2002), 285.

26. David S. Reynolds, *Mightier Than the Sword: "Uncle Tom's Cabin" and the Battle for America* (New York: W. W. Norton, 2011), 13.

27. Quoted in Henry Louis Gates Jr., "Introduction to The Annotated Uncle Tom's Cabin," in *The Annotated Uncle Tom's Cabin*, ed. Henry Louis Gates Jr. and Hollis Robbins (New York: W. W. Norton, 2007), xxix.

28. Hedrick, *Harriet Beecher Stowe*, 215; Jane Tompkins, "Sentimental Power: *Uncle Tom's Cabin* and the Politics of Literary History," in *Sensational Designs: The Cultural Work of American Fiction, 1790–1860* (New York: Oxford University Press, 1985), 147–48.

29. Tompkins, "Sentimental Power," 148. Tompkins draws on the interpretation of the jeremiad by Sacvan Bercovitch in his book *The American Jeremiad* (Madison: University of Wisconsin Press, 1978). According to Bercovitch, the jeremiad is "a mode of public exhortation . . . designed to join social criticism to spiritual renewal, public to private identity, the shifting 'signs of the times' to certain traditional metaphors, themes, and symbols." The purpose is "to direct an imperiled people toward the fulfillment of their destiny, to guide them individually toward salvation, and collectively toward the American city of God" (quoted in Tompkins, "Sentimental Power," 147–48).

30. Harriet Beecher Stowe, *The Minister's Wooing* (1859; reprint, Hartford, CT: Stowe-Day Foundation, 1988), 90.

trinal preaching, the women novelists sought to edify their readers through stories. And often women in the novels became the real preachers, offering a fresh and relevant gospel to hurting people, while the men tediously elaborated their doctrinal points one after another from their pulpits.

Cultural observers of the time recognized what the novelists were doing. Writer and critic Henry Tuckerman noted the role of popular fiction in spreading the gospel:

> In the pages of journals, in the verses of poets, in the favorite books of the hour we have homilies that teach charity and faith more eloquently than the conventional Sunday discourse; they come nearer to experience; they are more the offspring of earnest conviction, and therefore enlist popular sympathy.[31]

Similarly, though more pejoratively, Mark Twain noted that the gospel of Christ came "filtered down" to nineteenth-century Americans *"through the despised novel . . . and not from the drowsy pulpit."*[32]

In addition, as historian David S. Reynolds has argued, the popularity of these novels was one important influence on the turn from doctrine to narrative in the nineteenth-century pulpit. While there were many strands, including Black preaching, that contributed to the emergence of pulpit storytelling, popular, homiletical novels played a significant role. Phillips Brooks, for example, highlighted this influence in his Beecher Lectures. He approvingly recognized that the "competition of print has interfered very much . . . with the monotonous reiteration of commonplace abstractions" in the pulpit.[33] He further noted that the "statement of the subject, the divisions into heads, the recapitulation at the end, all the scaffolding and anatomy of a sermon is out of favor and there are many good jests about it."[34] In addition, in his lectures Henry Ward Beecher himself defended the edifying value of stories over the discussion of intricate details of doctrine.[35]

---

31. Quoted in Reynolds, *Faith in Fiction*, 209.
32. Reynolds, *Faith in Fiction*, 1.
33. Phillips Brooks, *On Preaching* (New York: Seabury Press, 1964), 12.
34. Brooks, *On Preaching*, 177–78.
35. Henry Ward Beecher, *Yale Lectures on Preaching*, 3 vols. (New York: Fords, Howard, and Hulbert, 1892), 3:306. Beecher also wrote a religious novel, *Norwood*, which, much to his chagrin, did not enjoy the success of his sister's works.

In light of this history, when I hear the term "New Homiletic" used to describe the turn to inductive and narrative preaching in the 1970s and 1980s, I want to say, "Really? A *new* homiletic? Don't limit the field to traditional pulpits. Some people weren't allowed to preach from them. Go back and listen to some women. Read Harriet Beecher Stowe and Susan Warner and Elizabeth Stuart Phelps." The New Homiletic wasn't so new after all. These women, many of them relegated to the backwaters of the literary canon by a male literary establishment, are some of its unsung heroes.[36]

Because Harriet Beecher Stowe preaches through *Uncle Tom's Cabin*, the time has come for a bit of sermon analysis. And every student of preaching knows how that goes. We begin with positive comments, though we all know a "but" is coming. Positively, Stowe's motivation is exemplary, and her homiletical strategy is significant. But in the end her white gaze and theological assumptions subvert many of her best intentions and serve as a warning to contemporary preachers. These appreciative and critical reflections are important. Both are a means of valuing the sermon and taking it seriously. So, as Rachel Maddow often says, "Stay with me."

Humanizing Stories: The Preacher's Dilemma

Through her sermon Stowe seeks directly to resist the weaponized grotesque embodied in the unjust political, legal, and economic system (that's her term—the system) of slavery.[37] Motivated by outrage at the system, Stowe shouts in the best way she can, "No, stop!" She tells stories that seek to open "hearts locked down as the lids of caskets." And in many ways she succeeded. When Stowe met Abraham Lincoln at the White House in 1862, the president is said to have greeted her with the comment, "So you're the little woman who wrote the book that started this great war!"[38] Even if Lincoln

---

36. Hedrick, *Harriet Beecher Stowe*, ix; Tompkins, "Sentimental Power," 132–35.
37. As Stowe writes in the preface to *Uncle Tom's Cabin*, "The object of these sketches is to awaken sympathy and feeling for the African race, as they exist among us; to show their wrongs and sorrows, under a system so necessarily cruel and unjust as to defeat and do away with the good effects of all that can be attempted for them, by their best friends, under it" (1).
38. Hedrick, *Harriet Beecher Stowe*, vii.

didn't literally say those words, the statement did reflect widespread popular opinion.[39] People were moved by Stowe's sermon, and her homiletical strategies are worth examining. In resisting the weaponized grotesque, she not only seeks to *humanize* those who have been labeled inhuman. She also proclaims Jesus' identification with the victims of the weaponized grotesque.

When *Uncle Tom's Cabin* was first advertised, the subtitle was not "Life among the Lowly"; rather it was "The Man That Was a Thing."[40] That subtitle captures Stowe's purpose. She sought to humanize people who had been grotesquely turned into things. That emphasis threads throughout the novel on virtually every page. And while she employs several strategies to accomplish this purpose, her primary means of doing this is unfortunately relevant today. Over and over again she depicts the wrenching separation of slave families, especially the separation of mothers from their children. And she graphically portrays the horrifying consequences of these separations. She creates a collision of narratives between the value of the domestic family at the heart of sentimental fiction and the breakup of slave families by their masters. That is an impressive homiletical strategy. Such a collision of narratives can often interrupt the status quo.[41]

One of the central plotlines involves the slave, Eliza, who risks her life to escape to Canada with her son, Harry, rather than being separated from him. More tragically, there is also the brief story of Lucy, who commits suicide by jumping off a boat into the river after her child is taken from her and sold.[42] And there is the extended story of Cassy, who, having had two children sold away from her, kills her third child rather than allowing him to grow up in slavery.[43] On page after page after page, Stowe depicts the wrenching *emotions* that these separations create in families—emotions that humanize people who were treated as things, as property, as chattel.[44] Moreover, Stowe

---

39. Reynolds, *Mightier Than the Sword*, x.
40. See Hollis Robbins, "Harriet Beecher Stowe and 'The Man That Was a Thing,'" in *The Annotated Uncle Tom's Cabin*, ed. Henry Louis Gates Jr. and Hollis Robbins (New York: W. W. Norton, 2007), xxxi–xlvii.
41. The problems with Stowe's use of this strategy are discussed below.
42. Stowe, *Uncle Tom's Cabin*, 107–12.
43. Stowe, *Uncle Tom's Cabin*, 303–12.
44. While emotions were a central feature of sentimental fiction and can be humanizing,

regularly cites Scripture against this evil, challenging the preachers of her time who used the Bible to support slavery. She also speaks directly to her readers to force identification with her characters. As Eliza begins her midnight escape with her son, Harry, Stowe writes,

> If it were *your* Harry, mother, or your Willie, that were going to be torn from you by a brutal trader, to-morrow morning,—if you had seen the man, and heard that papers were signed and delivered, and you had only from twelve o'clock till morning to make good your escape—how fast could *you* walk? How many miles could you make in those few brief hours?[45]

As in much sentimental fiction, there are tears, many tears. And they are meant to elicit the reader's tears in order to move people to empathy and action. Christine Smith has argued that preaching moves from weeping to confession to resistance.[46] Maybe Stowe was trying to do something similar. Empathy, Stowe recognizes, is one antidote to the weaponized grotesque—empathy that *may* lead to confession and resistance.

Stowe's novel calls to mind contemporary tears: tears shed at the southern border of the United States by parents and children separated from each other. We've heard the audio of that crying child; we've seen the photos. There were also the tears people shed when they saw images of asylum seekers torn from their children. Tears not just of sorrow, but of rage. Interesting, isn't it, that the separation of families finally caused people to wake up and take notice of the treatment of immigrants in this country—just like Stowe's depiction of the separation of slave families caused some people to wake up, open their hearts, and resist the weaponized grotesque that undergirded the system of slavery. "No, stop, they have histories, stories!"

In considering these tears, I became intrigued by some other tears I had read about. Four centuries earlier, at the beginning of the slave trade in Portugal, the royal chronicler Zurara shed tears while watching the auction of slaves who had just arrived in the country.

Stowe runs the risk of depicting Black people as primarily emotional—a racist stereotype that has been prevalent throughout history. Thanks to Donyelle McCray for calling this problem to my attention.

45. Stowe, *Uncle Tom's Cabin*, 43.

46. Christine M. Smith, *Preaching as Weeping, Confession, and Resistance: Radical Responses to Radical Evil* (Louisville, KY: Westminster/John Knox Press, 1992).

"Zurara's Tears" is the title of the opening chapter of theologian Willie Jennings's groundbreaking book *The Christian Imagination*.[47] Zurara's tears too were shed as he witnessed the separation of slave families. Those tears too implicitly acknowledged the humanity of people grotesquely treated as things or animals. But, as Jennings demonstrates, theological dogma, unquestioned colonialism, and a racial scale of being prevented Zurara from acting on his tears; he could not join and embrace those others. Apart from confession and resistance, tears alone are not enough. As Toni Morrison put it in her foreword to *The Bluest Eye*, people can take comfort in pity, rather than engaging in serious self-interrogation; people can be "touched, but not moved."[48]

With his reference to theological dogma, unquestioned colonialism, and a racial scale of being, Jennings points preachers to the larger context of personal stories that is essential for turning tears into confession and resistance. In her poem, Martinez points to this larger context through her comment, "they have *histories*" (italics added). Individual stories lead to confession and resistance when they point preachers back to the larger histories, systems, and ideologies that turn people into things. Stories—and the tears they may produce—cannot simply be approached individualistically; they are the consequence of centuries of political, economic, social— and theological—structures that have turned people into animals or things. Jennings calls preachers to move from tears to this kind of historical and structural analysis.

In her novel *The Bluest Eye*, Toni Morrison points her readers in a similar direction. She poignantly depicts the structural components, including the everyday violence, of a destructive ideology of beauty constructed and imposed by whiteness. At one point in the novel, in the midst of an argument, the wealthy, nicely dressed, light-skinned Maureen Peal proclaims herself cute and screams that Pecola, Frieda, and Claudia are "black and ugly."[49] Claudia, the narrator, experiencing a strange, new feeling of envy, reflects, "And all

---

47. Willie James Jennings, *The Christian Imagination: Theology and the Origins of Race* (New Haven, CT: Yale University Press, 2010), 15–64, esp. 15–24.

48. Toni Morrison, "Foreword," in *The Bluest Eye* (New York: Vintage International, 2007), xii.

49. Morrison, *Bluest Eye*, 73. For the description of the "enchanting" Maureen Peal, see pp. 62–63.

the time we knew that Maureen Peal was not the Enemy and not worthy of such intense hatred. The *Thing* to fear was the *Thing* that made *her* beautiful, and not us."[50] Morrison presents preachers with the larger issue to be addressed: what is the *Thing* that turns people into *things*? Unless tears push preachers back to a confrontation with this larger history—this larger *Thing*—tears don't necessarily lead to confession and resistance. People may simply be "touched, but not moved" by individual stories.[51]

Stories, Stowe reminds us, can humanize people and open hearts locked down like caskets. Preachers know that. But upon closer analysis, Stowe's novel also reminds us that telling these stories is complicated, and not only because they must direct us to address larger systems and ideologies. We preachers need to grapple with this complexity. Whenever people different from ourselves become victims of the weaponized grotesque, we confront the same challenge Stowe encountered. And this challenge includes not just racial differences but differences of any kind. In this situation, how do we tell humanizing stories?

Stowe's novel highlights the difficulties preachers face. Stowe reminds us of a kind of double-bind we are in. Our congregations need to hear stories that humanize victims of the weaponized grotesque. But it is very dangerous, even inappropriate, to tell another person's story. There is the danger of false patterns, the danger of misrepresentation. There is the hubris of presuming to speak for someone else—much less for another *group*. There is the problem of individualistic or sentimental sympathy that *ends* with tears. There is, in short, the problem of telling another person's story from our own

---

50. Morrison, *Bluest Eye*, 74.

51. My focus in this chapter is on the significance and challenge of telling humanizing stories. However, unmasking the systemic and ideological realities behind dehumanization is essential. I have examined these realities in Charles L. Campbell, *The Word before the Powers: An Ethic of Preaching* (Louisville, KY: Westminster John Knox Press, 2002). In addition to Jennings's analysis of the colonial and theological roots of race in the West, the following works analyze historically the political, economic, and ideological aspects of systemic racism in the United States, particularly the legal system's control of Black bodies: Barbara Jeanne Fields, "Slavery, Race, and Ideology in the United States of America," *New Left Review* 181 (May 1990): 95–118; Blackmon, *Slavery by Another Name*; Alexander, *New Jim Crow*. For a contemporary novel that uses a character's story to unmask the larger structures of racism through U.S. history, see Colson Whitehead, *The Underground Railroad* (New York: Doubleday, 2016).

perspective, as Stowe does by telling the stories of slaves from the perspective of an omniscient white narrator. Her gaze is sympathetic, but it remains a white gaze. Indeed, as has been the case throughout the period of European colonialism, the white gaze becomes the arbiter of what actually counts as human.

And that is the preacher's dilemma whenever we seek to tell another person's story; we cannot escape our own gaze, even with the best of intentions. Stowe was outraged by slavery, and she had to speak. But there were few outlets available to her; women had little recourse to act on their moral outrage, for "male professors, male clergy, [and] male politicians made the laws and shaped the public opinion of the land."[52] So Stowe did what she could do. She preached the abolitionist cause to countless people through her novel. And her novel shifted public opinion and moved many people to oppose slavery. As they critiqued aspects of the novel, even some prominent African Americans appreciated her efforts.[53]

More recently, however, critics have highlighted the "false patterns" imposed on slave lives by Stowe's white gaze. Angela Davis, for example, has argued that "the enormous influence [Stowe's] book enjoyed cannot compensate for its utter distortion of slave life."[54] In particular, Davis notes that Eliza, the central mother figure in *Uncle Tom's Cabin*, is a "travesty of the Black woman."[55] Through Stowe's homiletical strategy of highlighting the separation of Black families, she falsely imposes an ideal of *white* motherhood on the Black slave woman. She naively transposes "the mother-figure, praised by the

---

52. Hedrick, *Harriet Beecher Stowe*, 202.
53. Frederick Douglass, for example, was critical of aspects of the novel, such as Stowe's proposal for African colonization in Liberia, and was apparently the first person to use "Uncle Tom" as a symbol of weakness. Nevertheless, he engaged with Stowe and appreciated the novel. In his periodical *Frederick Douglass's Paper*, he praised the book, but also published criticisms of it. Despite his critique, Douglass apparently thought *Uncle Tom's Cabin* had the potential to do more good than harm. Moreover, Stowe listened to Douglass's criticisms and changed some of her positions. See Reynolds, *Mightier Than the Sword*, 118, 226, 255–56; Levine, "Introduction," xv–xvi; Robert S. Levine, "*Uncle Tom's Cabin* in Frederick Douglass' Paper: An Analysis of Reception," *American Literature* 64, no. 1 (1992): 71–93.
54. Angela Y. Davis, *Women, Race, and Class* (New York: Vintage Books, 1983), 27. Earlier James Baldwin also passionately criticized the novel for oversimplifying and misrepresenting the stories of slaves in racist ways. See James Baldwin, "Everybody's Protest Novel," in *Notes of a Native Son* (Boston: Beacon Press, 1955), 13–23. For a discussion of Stowe and Baldwin, see Gates, "Introduction to *The Annotated Uncle Tom's Cabin*."
55. Davis, *Women, Race, and Class*, 27.

cultural propaganda of the period, from white society to the slave community."⁵⁶ Eliza, Davis argues, "is white motherhood incarnate, but in blackface—or, rather, because she is a 'quadroon,' in a little-less-than-white face."⁵⁷

Stowe's central homiletical strategy sought to create empathy for Eliza among white women readers. And she succeeded. But that very strategy imposed a white gaze on Black women and distorted slave lives. Presenting Eliza through the lens of ideal white motherhood, Stowe creates an oddity "among the great majority of Black women."⁵⁸ In other words, Stowe presents Eliza, not as a particular person, but as a *type*—a figure of *white* motherhood. Eliza plays a role similar to that forced upon the character of Cora in Colson Whitehead's *The Underground Railroad*, who has to work as a *type* in a white-run museum about slave life.⁵⁹ As Cora portrays a slave woman in the museum, she knows her act falsifies her experience. A "false pattern" has been imposed upon Cora's story—a pattern Cora finds subtle ways to resist.⁶⁰ Similarly, Davis argues, Stowe's homiletical strategy, creative and successful as it was, imposed a false pattern—a false type—on slave women's experience. Stowe fails to depict Black women's "passionate abhorrence" to the realities and injustices of the slave system.⁶¹ As Davis concludes, "Because she accepts wholesale nineteenth-century mother worship, Stowe miserably fails to capture the reality and truth of Black women's resistance to slavery."⁶²

This is the dilemma of the preacher who seeks to use stories to humanize people who have been turned into animals or things. I have wrestled with this dilemma myself. A number of years ago, I coauthored a book titled *The Word on the Street*.⁶³ In the book my col-

---

56. Davis, *Women, Race, and Class*, 27.
57. Davis, *Women, Race, and Class*, 27.
58. Davis, *Women, Race, and Class*, 29.
59. Whitehead, *Underground Railroad*, see 107–17.
60. Cora gives the "evil eye" to patrons of the museum who looked at her. She reverses the "white gaze" by staring at specific patrons until they "broke," like a weak link in the chain. "It was a fine lesson, Cora thought, to learn that the slave, the African in your midst, is looking at you too" (Whitehead, *Underground Railroad*, 125–27).
61. Davis, *Women, Race, and Class*, 29.
62. Davis, *Women, Race, and Class*, 29.
63. Stanley P. Saunders and Charles L. Campbell, *The Word on the Street: Performing the Scriptures in the Urban Context* (2000; reprint, Eugene, OR: Wipf and Stock, 2006).

league Stan Saunders and I shared stories of homeless people whom we had encountered on the streets of Atlanta. We didn't take this task lightly. We had spent years on the streets getting to know people. We had eaten with them, slept on sidewalks with them, listened to them, and learned from them. We wanted their stories to be told. And readers have genuinely appreciated the book. But looking back, I wonder. Who was I—a comfortable, tenured professor—to tell *their* stories? How many false patterns did I impose on them? How often did I use them to support my own theological points? The words of Lucille Clifton's poem "why some people be mad at me sometime" trouble me:

> why some people be mad at me sometime
> they ask me to remember
> but they want me to remember
> their memories
> and I keep on remembering
> mine[64]

That is the preacher's dilemma. Other people's stories, other people's memories, are not ours to tell. But we are called to resist the weaponized grotesque, and sharing stories is an effective way to do that. We cannot escape the dilemma. And we will never get it just right. But we *can* be careful. We can listen deeply to others before we speak. We can get to know people and invite them to edit and approve not only the stories we tell, but the way we use them. We can avoid treating people as *types*. We can be self-critical about the ways in which our perspective inevitably colors the stories we tell; we can confess that in our sermons themselves. We can examine the ways these stories direct us to larger oppressive systems and ideologies. But best of all, we can at times turn over our pulpits to others so that they can tell their own stories, provide their own descriptions, and share their own memories, even if some people get mad sometime.

---

64. Lucille Clifton, "why some people be mad at me sometime," in *Blessing the Boats: New and Selected Poems, 1998–2000* (Rochester, NY: BOA Editions, 2000), 38.

Jesus, the Man That Was a Thing

Stowe doesn't simply tell other persons' stories. At a deeper level, she is telling the story of Jesus. By making Tom a Christ figure she proclaims Jesus' identification with the victims of the weaponized grotesque. Interestingly, as Willie Jennings details, Zurara inadvertently does the same thing. Praying in response to the slave auction, Zurara interrupts the colonial narrative and figures the experience of the slaves through the passion narrative.[65] In Jennings's words, Zurara "joins the slave body to the body of Jesus."[66] Those treated as property—chattel—actually become Christ figures. As Jennings notes, however, Zurara's Christology is neither salvific nor life-giving; it leads only to death because Zurara cannot imagine the full implications of what he is doing.[67] But I am intrigued that at the "origins of race," as Jennings puts it, Zurara inadvertently hints at the humanizing, Christologizing moves that an abolitionist in the United States will use centuries later in seeking to *end* slavery. It makes the racist theological history that Jennings recounts seem all the more tragic.

Stowe also "joins the slave body to the body of Jesus," though she does so intentionally, rather than inadvertently. Tom, "the man that was a thing," becomes the Christ figure, whose passion narrative begins when he is sold to the cruel master, Simon Legree. Importantly, during his passion, Tom is not simply a passive Christ figure, but is more defiant than he is often given credit for being. On more than one occasion, Tom refuses to follow Legree's demands. Asserting his own humanity, Tom will not act against his conscience, and he is beaten more than once for his resistance. Finally, after encouraging the slaves Cassy and Emmeline to escape, Tom refuses to reveal where they are hiding, even though he tauntingly tells Legree he knows exactly where they are.[68] Tom could have avoided death if he had just obeyed Legree and betrayed the women. But he refuses, and he literally saves Cassy and Emmeline. Tom is killed because he defies the master. And Stowe makes the link to Jesus clear. Along his via dolorosa, Tom sees a vision of "One crowned with thorns,

---

65. Jennings, *Christian Imagination*, 20–22.
66. Jennings, *Christian Imagination*, 22.
67. Jennings, *Christian Imagination*, 20–23.
68. Stowe, *Uncle Tom's Cabin*, 348–49.

buffeted and bleeding," but also crowned with glory and splendor.[69] Tom has his moment of doubt, asking if God has forsaken him. He remembers Jesus' last days, and repeats Jesus' words: "Into thy hands I commend my spirit." He forgives his enemies and proclaims a gospel of love.[70] And people are changed by his death.

Stowe's move here is scandalous. What an offense it must have been to join the slave body to the body of Jesus. According to the norms of many of her readers, the combination of slave-Christ, thing-Christ must have seemed grotesque. Stowe engages in radical, destabilizing pairings of opposites. Stowe subverts binary categories and creates disruptive incongruities. No wonder many people who benefited from the binaries hated the book.

Stowe's novel actually takes us back to the *Alexamenos graffito*, which I discussed in chapter 1: Jesus becomes the object of animalistic and objectifying dehumanization. Tom is the Christ figure, yes. But Jesus is refigured here as well. Jesus becomes the victim of the weaponized grotesque, which is a profound insight into the gospel. For surely that *was* the case for one crucified. The person became a nonhuman thing—an object. A means of deterrence. Something to be laughed at on the cross. As in the *Alexamenos graffito*, Jesus becomes the divine-human-*nonhuman* one. Jesus himself becomes "the man that was a thing."

Stowe declares Jesus' identification with those who have been dehumanized. And in that way she seeks *theologically* to resist the weaponized grotesque—to say, in God's name, "No, stop." It is a bold move.

Despite Stowe's bold insights, however, she presents preachers with a troubling theological challenge. Depicting other people as Christ figures is dangerous.[71] These depictions always bring with them theological assumptions. They inevitably impose a theological pattern on another person or group, who may want no part of it. That is what happens in the novel. I think it is one reason the book is so troubling for many of us. Stowe imposes a theological pattern on

---

69. Stowe, *Uncle Tom's Cabin*, 330.
70. Stowe, *Uncle Tom's Cabin*, 345–50.
71. More broadly, treating people as theological types, which Stowe does throughout the novel, is dangerous. Human experiences are forced into imposed patterns. On *Uncle Tom's Cabin* as a "typological narrative," see Tompkins, "Sentimental Power," 131–53.

Tom's brutal suffering and death; he becomes a figure of redemptive suffering. His death saves others. Because of her particular sacrificial theology, which was pervasive in her culture, that is the way Stowe can "join the slave body to the body of Jesus."[72] But in so doing, she reminds us that the *theological* gaze can be as dangerous as the *racial* gaze.[73]

Which raises important questions for all of us preachers. Is it appropriate for Stowe to declare a *slave's* suffering at the hands of the white master to be redemptive? Would it ever be appropriate for *me* to pronounce an oppressed group's suffering to be redemptive? Indeed, is it ever appropriate for *any of us* to claim that another person's or another group's suffering is redemptive? I don't think so. Such imposed christological patterns, in Jennings's words, may be neither salvific nor life-giving. It would be like telling Gregory Orr after he killed his brother, "Your suffering is beautiful; it will surely save others." Even employed with the best of intentions, Christ figures can simply be another way to impose dangerous, false patterns that ignore the complex experience of the ones on whom they are imposed. When the pattern imposed is redemptive suffering, it can even validate and perpetuate the suffering of oppressed people.

In his book *The Cross and the Lynching Tree*, James Cone takes us more deeply into the unsettling relationship between the story of Jesus and the weaponized grotesque. Lynchings are the extreme American grotesque. People are treated as animals or things in a spectacle of death carried out with the grotesque incongruities of horror and laughter, repulsiveness and celebration. And the fears and justifications that drove lynchings were the same as those that led to the writing of "Murders in the Rue Morgue."

It is hard to imagine a more brutal expression of the weaponized grotesque than a lynching—except, Cone suggests, for crucifixion. Indeed, linking the cross and the lynching tree, Cone argues, requires

---

72. As Tompkins has demonstrated, the novel is shaped by a theology of redemptive suffering. The drama "of which all the major episodes of the novel are transformations [is] the idea, central to Christian soteriology, that the highest human calling is to give one's life for another." This pervasive cultural myth "invests the suffering and death of an innocent victim with just the kind of power that critics deny to Stowe's novel: the power to work in, and change, the world" (Tompkins, "Sentimental Power," 136, 138).

73. Indeed, as Willie Jennings has persuasively argued in *The Christian Imagination*, the racial gaze and the theological gaze have often been inseparable through the centuries.

imagination—imagination rooted in the realities of experience, rather than theological abstractions. White academic theologians, Cone claims, *lacked* the imagination to see the connection between the cross and the lynching tree.[74] Artists are needed, he writes, "for us to see things we do not want to look at because they make us uncomfortable with ourselves and the world we have created."[75] Cone therefore does not try to explain the saving power of the cross; he does not try to impose a pattern. Instead, he recognizes it as a "mystery, beyond human understanding and control."[76] He does not try to untangle or resolve the grotesque contradictions. Rather, he writes, "The cross is a reminder that the world is fraught with many contradictions, many lynching trees."[77]

For Cone, this grotesque juxtaposition of the cross and the lynching tree is the scandal of the gospel. Listen to what he says:

> The lynching tree is the cross in America. When American Christians realize that they can meet Jesus only in the crucified bodies in our midst, they will encounter the real scandal of the cross. . . . The real scandal of the gospel is this: humanity's salvation is revealed in the cross of the condemned criminal Jesus, and humanity's salvation is available *only* through our solidarity with crucified people in our midst. Faith that emerged out of the scandal of the cross is not a faith of intellectuals or elites of any sort. This is the faith of abused and scandalized people—the losers and the down and out. . . . Any genuine theology and any genuine preaching of the Christian gospel must be measured against the test of the scandal of the cross and the lynching tree.[78]

Cone doesn't try to explain the contradictions of a grotesque gospel. Rather, he sets us down in a U.S. sanctuary like the one in San Salvador. At the front there is a beautiful, colorful cross, and there are striking images of hope. But on the back wall are the stations of the cross—only now they are graphic images of lynchings. In between, facing those images, sits the pulpit. And from that pulpit, where we can never avoid the weaponized grotesque, we preach: "No, stop!"

---

74. James Cone, *The Cross and the Lynching Tree* (Maryknoll, NY: Orbis, 2011), 30ff.
75. Cone, *Cross and the Lynching Tree*, 117.
76. Cone, *Cross and the Lynching Tree*, 74.
77. Cone, *Cross and the Lynching Tree*, 159.
78. Cone, *Cross and the Lynching Tree*, 158–61.

Chapter 3

Incarnate Word

Preaching and the Carnivalesque Grotesque

*T*he Word became grotesque and dwelt among us. That is my own paraphrase of John 1:14. I haven't seen that translation in any of the versions I've checked, but I think it's appropriate. The Word became grotesque and dwelt among us. The Word that was *God* became *flesh* and dwelt among us. God-flesh. John proclaims a paradoxical anomaly that transgresses our binary categories and subverts the norms of human and divine. Jesus' fleshy divine body is almost a classic definition of the grotesque. The Word became grotesque and dwelt among us.

Grotesque Realism

Beyond this irresolvable incongruity—God-flesh—the incarnate Word takes us even more deeply into the grotesque. For the grotesque engages in *degradation*. But degradation here is not a negative term. It involves bringing down to earth all that is high and lifted up, including heaven itself. Mikhail Bakhtin calls this "grotesque realism." He writes, "The essential principle of grotesque realism is degradation, that is, the lowering of all that is high, spiritual, ideal, abstract; it is a transfer to the material level, to the sphere of earth and body."[1] "Degradation here means coming down to earth."[2] The Word became grotesque and dwelt among us.

---

1. Mikhail Bakhtin, *Rabelais and His World*, trans. Helene Iswolsky (Bloomington: Indiana University Press, 1984), 19.
2. Bakhtin, *Rabelais and His World*, 21.

Grotesque realism is the carnivalesque grotesque. The root of *carn*-ival is the same as in-*carn*-ation. Like the body of Jesus, carnival enacts the grotesque. It degrades all that is high and lifted up. It brings down the abstract, the idealized, the ethereal and gives them bodily form. It enacts the Word made flesh. It *performs* incarnation. Accordingly, carnival scandalously celebrates the *lower* body, with all of its reproductive, digestive, and excretory functions. That description is actually a sanitized version of what I'm talking about: sex, eating and drinking, urinating and defecating. The daily realities of human flesh. Carnival both acknowledges and celebrates our creatureliness—the fleshy, material dimension of human life that piety and manners and pulpits often seek to deny or control.[3] To borrow Paul's words from 1 Corinthians 12:23–24, carnival clothes with greater honor those members of the body we think less honorable. It treats with greater respect our less respectable members. It gives the greater honor to the inferior members of the body. Paul-carnival. Now that's a destabilizing pair of opposites.

Carnival, then, is not simply a raucous celebration; it is profoundly theological. It brings *theology* down to earth. It enfleshes our theological claims about an incarnate God. Words about God become grotesque and dwell among us. Carnival celebrates a God "who chooses muddy flesh over homiletic word."[4] Indeed, when sermons were preached during carnival, they were generally mock sermons. There's a long tradition of these sermons. "Dreary beloved," one begins. They often celebrate impious saints like Saint Ham and Saint Sausage and even Saint Nobody. And they scandalously celebrate human flesh and the functions of the lower body.[5] Carnival and the carnivalesque represent a profound theological tradition that offers "a more radical reading of the Christian narrative" than is generally

---

3. Bakhtin develops the relationship between carnival and the grotesque body throughout *Rabelais and His World*. See also Edward Muir, "Carnival and the Lower Body," in *Ritual in Early Modern Europe* (Cambridge: Cambridge University Press, 1997), 85–116; and Max Harris, *Carnival and Other Christian Festivals: Folk Theology and Folk Performance* (Austin: University of Texas Press, 2003).

4. Harris, *Carnival*, 224.

5. See Ben Parsons and Bas Jongenelen, "'The Sermon on Saint Nobody': A Verse Translation of a Middle Dutch Parodic Sermon," *Journal of American Folklore* 123, no. 487 (2010): 92–107; Jelle Koopmans, *Quatre Sermons Joyeux* (Geneva: Droz, 1984); Malcolm Jones, "The Parodic Sermon in Medieval and Early Modern England," *Medium Aevum* 66, no. 1 (1997): 90–114.

heard from pulpits or liturgies or academies.⁶ Yet I confess, while I've explored carnival a few times in my classes, I have rarely discussed its *theological* insights. And I've never required my students to preach a mock sermon. In my teaching I have generally ignored this important tradition.

Maybe many of us have ignored the carnivalesque because of our rage for order. Carnival is not orderly. It celebrates the matter—the flesh—that we might prefer to exclude from our churches and our pulpits. And again, artists often must remind us of our exclusions. Consider Andres Serrano's photograph *Immersion* (*Piss Christ*), which has been cited as an example of the artistic carnivalesque.⁷ It is a photograph of a crucifix—a cheap, plastic Jesus on a wooden cross—submerged in a jar of urine. A commodified Jesus is immersed—baptized?—in lower-body material. We cannot view Christ except through the excretions of the human body. The image is in many ways repulsive, but it is also strangely beautiful and mysterious. Paradoxically, the cheap crucifix is transformed in the urine. The crucified Jesus is bathed in a reddish-golden light. The photograph "is both ominous and glorious."⁸ The Word became grotesque and dwelt among us, "and we have seen his glory," as the Gospel of John puts it (1:14).

But the photograph created a scandal. It was considered offensive—blasphemous. Serrano received death threats and hate mail. U.S. senators attacked the National Endowment for the Arts, which had supported Serrano's art. This Jesus did not fit into the ideal patterns of Christian beauty or piety. The photograph disturbed purity and order. It was grotesque.⁹

---

6. Harris, *Carnival*, 144.

7. Lewis Hyde, *Trickster Makes This World: Mischief, Myth, and Art* (New York: North Point Press, 1998), 191–94.

8. Lucy R. Lippard, "Andres Serrano: The Spirit and the Letter," *Art in America* 78 (April 1990): 239. Serrano's own relationship to Christianity, like his photography, actually has the characteristics of the grotesque. Serrano's works "reveal both his conflicted relationship with the church and the way he is drawn to Christianity. The artist explores his spiritual doubts, . . . seeking both to express and to resolve the paradox he feels, torn between fascination and repulsion" (Nathalie Dietschy, "From Urine to the Hammer: Andres Serrano and the Stigmata of Scandal," in *Andres Serrano: Uncensored Photographs* [Brussels: Royal Museums of Fine Arts of Belgium, 2016], 36).

9. The photograph was vandalized in 1997 and again in 2011. But Serrano stated, "I am appalled by the claim of 'anti-Christian bigotry' that has been attributed to my picture *Piss Christ*. The photograph, and the title itself, are ambiguously provocative, but certainly not blasphemous" (quoted in Dietschy, "From Urine to the Hammer," 37).

That's just the point. The Word became grotesque and dwelt among us. As cultural critic Lewis Hyde has noted, *Piss Christ* affirms "that Christ's incarnation is key to the Gospels, that the crucifix should remind us that his *body* suffered on the cross. When he wept there were tears; the thorns and spears drew blood. The whole story falls apart if none of that matters, if a purified Christ is a fleshless Christ."[10] So, in the photograph we see the crucifix through the body. The dead Christ has a shroud of urine. The photograph, Hyde comments, joins an abstracted Christ and the human body, specifically the waste from which we normally avert our eyes.[11]

That is the work of carnival and the carnivalesque. The festivities remind us that an "overpurified Christ" may not have much to offer the complexity of our fleshy lives,[12] which raises some questions: How do we preachers overpurify Christ through our piety and manners? Through our false patterns? What aspects of our complex, fleshy lives have been excluded from our sermons and our churches because of our idealization of the gospel? What bodily realities have become taboo because of our rage for order? The Word became grotesque and dwelt among us. Too often I have averted my eyes. Maybe some of you have too.

It should not be surprising that carnival celebrations originally began at Christmas. Jesus' bloody, watery birth turned the world upside down. Moreover, Mary became a key figure for carnival, not simply by giving birth to Jesus, but also through her Magnificat.[13] Just as Jesus' birth turned the world upside down, so did Mary's preaching. While she was pregnant, Mary raised her voice in what Óscar Romero called "holy defiance":[14]

> My soul magnifies the Lord,
>   and my spirit rejoices in God my Savior,
> for he has looked with favor on the lowliness of his servant.
> . . . .
>   [The Lord] has scattered the proud in the thoughts of their hearts.

---

10. Hyde, *Trickster Makes This World*, 192.
11. Hyde, *Trickster Makes This World*, 192.
12. Hyde, *Trickster Makes This World*, 181.
13. Harris, *Carnival*, 25–27, 140–41, 153, 222–24.
14. Óscar Romero, "I Bring You Great News: A Saviour Has Been Born to You!," December 24, 1979, http://www.romerotrust.org.uk/homilies-and-writings/homilies/i-bring-you-great-news-saviour-has-been-born-you, p. 3.

> He has brought down the powerful from their thrones,
>   and lifted up the lowly;
> he has filled the hungry with good things,
>   and sent the rich away empty.
>
> Luke 1:46–53

Mary provides the template for carnival. Carnival is the embodied theology of the marginalized that brings down the powerful from their thrones and lifts up the lowly. It is the theology of those who are the lower-body politic. And it is celebratory; it is a festival of freedom and laughter. As Wynona Judd sang, "We could use a revolution. The world is turned upside down. Let's make a baby king."[15] That is the spirit of carnival. It is a festive performance of folk theology that subverts hierarchies, including ecclesial hierarchies and official theology. Through carnival those who have been marginalized enact in bodily form their resistance to the oppressive norms of the status quo.

The goal is not simply negative or destructive. Carnival brings down the old so that the new might be born, just as Jesus' birth and Mary's song interrupt the old order with a new creation. The grotesque realism of carnival celebrates "the potentiality of another world, another order, another way of life."[16] In carnival, we might say, people who know all too well the horrific stations of the cross at the back of the sanctuary nevertheless look toward the front; they celebrate and perform the colorful, lively images of promise and hope. And the festivals were not simply an escapist safety valve for the oppressed, giving them a momentary outlet, but ultimately reinforcing the powers that be. Rather, as has been widely documented, these festivities frequently led to ongoing practices of resistance and even to revolutionary change.[17]

That is the character of carnival's grotesque realism: Christ dwells among the fleshy complexities of human life. The festival brings heaven down to earth. It brings down the high and lifts up the lowly.

---

15. Wynona Judd, "Let's Make a Baby King," *Tell Me Why*, MCA Nashville, 1993.
16. Bakhtin, *Rabelais and His World*, 230.
17. See, for example, James C. Scott, *Domination and the Arts of Resistance: Hidden Transcripts* (New Haven, CT: Yale University Press, 1990), 172–82; Natalie Zemon Davis, "Women on Top," in *Society and Culture in Early Modern France* (Stanford, CA: Stanford University Press, 1975), 124–51.

It performs the potentiality of another world. But the carnivalesque grotesque runs even deeper, for this celebration of those on the margins enacts what Bakhtin calls the *grotesque body*. That takes us to the deepest and most profound insight into the carnivalesque grotesque, with important implications for preaching, homiletics, and the church.

The Grotesque Body

Bakhtin distinguishes the grotesque body from the classical body.[18] The classical body is an entirely finished, limited body, with clear and sharp boundaries around it. It smoothes out the protuberances and cavities of the body and closes itself against the surrounding world.[19] Today we might say it's the hard, sculpted body, with its taut and rigid boundaries—the body celebrated in the media from magazines to films to television.

In contrast to the classical body, there is the grotesque body. It's the body in the act of becoming. It is never finished, never completed, but continually growing and created; and it also grows and creates other bodies—thus the emphasis on those parts of the body that engage and interact with other bodies and the surrounding world. We breathe through our protruding noses—and in the process we are profoundly connected with others, though we rarely think about that. We are all breathing each other's air, for example; none of us is an isolated individual. We eat and drink from the earth, taking the earth into our bodies. And when we defecate and urinate, our waste returns to the earth and even fertilizes it for new growth. Most of us have sex at some point, connecting ourselves to others; many menstruate, some give birth and breastfeed, all part of the process of procreation. We die and return to the earth—from dust to dust—which continues to generate new life. The grotesque body is never a finished body; it is never demarcated against other bodies or the earth. The grotesque body is generative, always transgressing its own boundaries.

---

18. For Bakhtin's extensive treatment of the grotesque body, see *Rabelais and His World*, 303–436.
19. Ola Sigurdson, "The Christian Body as a Grotesque Body," in *Embodiment in Cognition and Culture*, ed. John Michael Krois et al. (Amsterdam: John Benjamins, 2007), 254.

It is a social body, part of a people who are continually growing and changing.[20]

For the grotesque body, the drama takes place at the *margins* of the body, as these margins are transgressed—just as when we breathe and eat and have sex and defecate and urinate the margins of our bodies are transgressed. The grotesque body is the body of the sweating, spitting preacher described by Donyelle McCray in her important article, "Sweating, Spitting, and Cursing: Intimations of the Sacred."[21] Her article depicts an appropriately grotesque degradation of the sacred—the Word made flesh indeed.

Mary Russo has concisely summarized these two kinds of bodies:

> The classical body is transcendent and monumental, closed, static, self-contained, symmetrical, and sleek; it is identified with the "high" or official culture of the Renaissance and later, with rationalism, individualism, and the normalizing aspirations of the bourgeoisie. The grotesque body is open, protruding, irregular, secreting, multiple, and changing; it is identified with the non-official, "low" culture or the carnivalesque, with social transformation.[22]

The grotesque body of carnival provides an alternative to the weaponized grotesque that I discussed in chapter 2. As I have noted, the grotesque body is a constantly changing body. It does not fear transitions or seek rigid boundaries; it does not build walls. Rather, it lives at the margins, in the interactions with other bodies, different bodies. There is no fear of change and transition; that's the very character of the grotesque body's life. It is dynamic, open, changing. That's what carnival is all about: the dying of the old, oppressive structures so that a new, dynamic whole may be born. Rigid boundaries and the weaponized grotesque have no place there. On certain carnivalesque feast days, in the church's liturgy itself, a child becomes the bishop. Both men and women engage in cross-dressing. Congregants bray like donkeys. Dung is burned as incense. Binaries and boundaries

---

20. Bakhtin, *Rabelais and His World*, 19.
21. Donyelle McCray, "Sweating, Spitting, and Cursing: Intimations of the Sacred," *Practical Matters* 9 (April 2015): 62–72.
22. Mary Russo, *The Female Grotesque: Risk, Excess and Modernity* (New York: Routledge, 1994), 8.

explode.[23] As Russo writes, "The grotesque body was exuberantly and democratically open and inclusive of all possibilities. Boundaries between individuals and society, between genders, between species, and between classes were blurred or brought into crisis in the inversions and hyperbole of carnivalesque representation."[24]

In addition, the grotesque body of carnival is not an objectified body; it is not subject to an external gaze. There is no audience in carnival. It is not a theatrical performance put on for spectators. Everyone participates. Everyone is part of the performance. There is no place for animalistic dehumanization. No one there becomes a thing. The weaponized grotesque has no home there, for nobody is an object. All are part of "an incomplete but imaginable wholeness."[25]

This is the deepest sense in which the Word became grotesque and dwelt among us. For Jesus is not simply the Word made flesh, as paradoxical as that is. Rather, Jesus is the Word made a grotesque body. This reality runs throughout the Gospels. But consider first one story from Mark—the story traditionally titled "the woman with the flow of blood." In her remarkable interpretation of this story Candida Moss highlights the grotesque character of Jesus' body. Her article is titled "The Man with the Flow of Power: Porous Bodies in Mark 5:25–34."[26] Although Moss doesn't use the phrase "grotesque body," she beautifully describes the dynamic. Both the body of the woman and the body of Jesus are porous, leaky bodies—grotesque, carnivalesque bodies. In that culture, the hot, dry, firm, impenetrable body (like the classical body) was the ideal.[27] Over against that norm *both* the woman *and* Jesus appear weak and sickly. The woman leaks blood; she does not control her bodily boundaries. But, similarly, Jesus leaks power; he also does not control *his* bodily boundaries. When the woman touches his cloak, power goes out from him. Power leaks from his body, and he feels it. But he does not control it. As Moss writes, "Jesus cannot control his own emissions." Rather,

---

23. Harris, *Carnival*, 140–42.
24. Russo, *Female Grotesque*, 79.
25. Russo, *Female Grotesque*, 78.
26. Candida Moss, "The Man with the Flow of Power: Porous Bodies in Mark 5:25–34," *Journal of Biblical Literature* 129, no. 3 (2010): 507–19. My discussion of this text relies on Moss's article.
27. See also Brittany E. Wilson, *Unmanly Men: Refigurations of Masculinity in Luke–Acts* (New York: Oxford University Press, 2015), 39–78.

the woman controls them. "The woman pulls divine power out of the passive, leaky Jesus."[28]

As Moss interprets it, this is a story of grotesque bodies. Neither the woman's body nor Jesus' body is self-contained, finished, or individual. They are inescapably social bodies, transgressive bodies, crossing boundaries in a generative process of death and renewal. Indeed, in the process the cultural norms of male and female bodies are also subverted; gender binaries are blurred and disrupted in the interaction. The drama takes place, not in some isolated center of a self-contained, individual body, but at the *margins* of the bodies, in their interaction with each other. That is the unfinished, in-between place where rebirth and renewal happen in the story. And in that encounter the "weak" and porous body of Jesus paradoxically leaks *power*. Weak power. Mark resorts to a destabilizing pair of opposites to characterize the grotesque body of Jesus.

The story has still another carnivalesque dimension. As in Mary's Magnificat, the world here is turned upside down. The woman's body is disruptively out of place. She's considered unclean. She shouldn't be in the crowd. And she certainly shouldn't be touching Jesus. As Russo argues,

> The marginal position of women and others in the "indicative" world makes their presence in the "subjunctive" or possible world of the topsy-turvy carnival "quintessentially" dangerous. . . . In other words, in the everyday indicative world, women and their bodies, certain bodies, in certain public framings, in certain public spaces, are always already transgressive—dangerous and in danger.[29]

The woman in the crowd is disorderly and dangerous. Her body can make others unclean. So the crowd is not a safe place for her. That's an often overlooked and disturbing dimension of carnival. We have to be honest about it. The possible world of carnival was not always a safe space for women; they could be assaulted there.[30] In the swirl of the topsy-turvy carnival, bodily boundaries could be inappropriately violated. For women, stepping out of their given, subordinate

---

28. Moss, "Flow of Power," 516–17.
29. Russo, *Female Grotesque*, 60.
30. Russo, *Female Grotesque*, 60.

roles could be dangerous. Bakhtin's interpretation of carnival does not represent a simple historical reality, but more an eschatological vision. Carnival performs an *incomplete*, but imaginable wholeness.

To greatly oversimplify, Russo's point is this: for women, the carnivalesque grotesque means not just bringing the high low, but making the low high.[31] As Mary proclaimed, the world is turned upside down; the norms are reversed. So Russo's primary images of the female carnivalesque are the airplane pilot and the trapeze artist, high and lifted up, but in a precarious position.[32] Like many women who step into the pulpit.

Such is the woman in Mark 5. She's out of her place, breaking norms; she's in a risky, dangerous position. But in her encounter with Jesus, a radical reversal takes place. The low becomes high. The woman exerts power over the body of the man. And even more than that, as Moss writes, "the *disabled* woman *ably* controls the body of the spiritual and physical physician."[33] The patient-physician relationship is upended. And importantly, after the healing, Jesus *listens* to the woman—he listens as she shares her truth for the entire crowd to hear. And he believes her. Then he praises her. The crowd becomes a safe space. The dynamics of the grotesque body are all enacted in this narrative. In this encounter, at the margins of those two bodies, Jesus' hidden divine identity is revealed.[34] The weak power of God moves through Jesus' porous, leaky body. The Word became grotesque and dwelt among us.

Jesus' grotesque body is evident throughout the Gospels, not simply in this one story. The boundaries of his body are never closed or static. He is a porous, leaky person. He sweats blood; he weeps; he spits and rubs his saliva on people to heal them; he touches the untouchables. And on the cross his body is pierced and bleeds; it is naked and open to the world. Even in resurrection Jesus' body is a grotesque body, where the wounds that open him to others remain present, touchable. There are no closed, static boundaries to Jesus' body. As theologian Frederick Bauerschmidt has written, "Christ's

---

31. Russo, *Female Grotesque*, 144, 154.
32. Russo, *Female Grotesque*, 17–51.
33. Moss, "Flow of Power," 516 (italics added).
34. Moss, "Flow of Power," 519.

body is a body of flesh that desires our flesh, that indeed is shattered in desire for us, a body moist and labile, generative and mutative. This is the home God has prepared for humanity."[35] The Word became grotesque and dwelt among us.

We celebrate this very body at our Eucharistic feast. Once again Jesus shares his body with us. We eat his flesh. We drink his blood. And his body works its way through us and returns to the earth to fertilize it for new birth. Our feast is grotesque not because eating flesh and drinking blood sounds gross; not because the meal is a form of cannibalism. Rather, our feast is grotesque because it remembers and celebrates the grotesque body of Jesus—leaking, open, shared with us. And the meal calls *the church* to be the grotesque Body of Christ.

Which brings us to the carnivalesque preaching of the Russian punk rock performance group Pussy Riot.[36] On February 21, 2012, at the beginning of the Russian Orthodox carnival season called Maslenitsa, several members of the group entered Christ the Savior Cathedral in Moscow. They invaded the seat of the patriarch of the Russian Orthodox Church, "the most visible Russian location of power and sacred space."[37] In their colorful miniskirts and tights and balaclavas, they entered the *ambo*, the space of preaching, a space reserved for men, and they performed their Punk Prayer: "Mother of God, Put Putin Away." As theologian Nicholas Denysenko has demonstrated, the prayer drew on a long history of appeals to Mary as the protector of the Russian people. And the prayer employed a choral refrain using a traditional and beloved liturgical hymn to

---

35. Frederick Christian Bauerschmidt, *Julian of Norwich and the Mystical Body Politic of Christ* (Notre Dame: University of Notre Dame, 1999), 107, quoted in Sigurdson, "Christian Body as a Grotesque Body," 255.

36. My treatment of Pussy Riot relies primarily on Nicholas Denysenko, "An Appeal to Mary: An Analysis of Pussy Riot's Punk Performance in Moscow," *Journal of the American Academy of Religion* 81, no. 4 (December 2013): 1061–92. See also Masha Gessen, *Words Will Break Cement: The Passion of Pussy Riot* (New York: Riverhead Books, 2014); Feminist Press, *Pussy Riot! A Punk Prayer for Freedom* (New York: Feminist Press, 2013); Maria Alyokhina, Yekaterina Samutsevich, and Nadezhda Tolokonnikova, "Pussy Riot Closing Statements," *n+1*, August 8, 2012, https://nplusonemag.com/online-only/online-only/pussy-riot-closing-statements/; Timothy Beal, "Pussy Riot's Theology," *Chronicle of Higher Education*, September 17, 2012, https://www.chronicle.com/article/Pussy-Riots-Theology/134398; Kerith M. Woodyard, "Pussy Riot and the Holy Foolishness of Punk," *Rock Music Studies* 1, no. 3 (2014): 268–86. To view the performance, see https://www.youtube.com/watch?v=lPDkJbTQRCY.

37. Denysenko, "An Appeal to Mary," 1063.

Mary from Rachmaninov's *Vigil*, though the women substituted their own subversive lyrics: "Mother of God, put Putin away, put Putin away, put Putin away." "Virgin Mary, Mother of God, become a feminist, become a feminist, become a feminist."[38] During these refrains they prostrated themselves and performed traditional signs of the cross.

Between the refrains, they shifted into punk rock and raucously danced. Costumes and dancing, as they later noted, are characteristics of the Russian Orthodox carnival.[39] In the verses they challenged the corruption of the ecclesial hierarchy and condemned the church's collaboration with Putin. They challenged the way in which the patriarch had brought a relic of Mary to Moscow and used it to undergird the status quo and align the church with the government. They denounced the treatment of women and protestors and LGBTQ+ persons. And, in classic, lower-body carnival fashion, they condemned all of these abuses as the Lord's "shit." "Believe in God, not in Putin," they proclaimed. And they claimed Mary, the protector of Russia, as the supporter of protest in the country.

The performance lasted just a couple of minutes. There was chaos before the women were run out of the church. But they filmed the performance, added some material recorded at another church, dubbed it with the music, and put it out on social media. It went viral. As you might imagine, it created a scandal. Women's bodies in a holy space reserved for men—the space of *preaching*. A brazen hybrid performance mixing the sacred and the profane. Immodest, colorful costumes and dancing. Vulgar language—even the word "feminist" was considered a curse word in that context.[40] The performance was offensive to many—blasphemous. Even the name of the group offended. Three of the women were arrested and convicted of "hooliganism motivated by religious hatred." Two of them served almost two years in prison. They were women out of place and dangerous. But the performance was also inspiring and empowering to many, and the women garnered countless supporters in Russia and around the world.

---

38. The translations of the prayer are taken from Denysenko, "An Appeal to Mary."
39. Feminist Press, *Pussy Riot!*, 39.
40. Feminist Press, *Pussy Riot!*, 50.

Preaching and the Carnivalesque Grotesque   53

The criticisms of the women echoed criticisms of the carnivalesque by those in power throughout history. In March 1445, for example, the Faculty of Theology at the University of Paris issued a letter to the bishops of France, deploring clerical behavior during popular festivals. They wrote, "Priests and clerks may be seen wearing masks and monstrous visages at the hours of office. They dance in the choir dressed as women, panders, or minstrels. They sing wanton songs. . . . They run and leap through the church, without blush at their own shame."[41]

Many interpreters, including Denysenko, have interpreted Pussy Riot's performance through the lens of the holy fools—those bizarre and often obscene figures who scandalized the piety of the church. They wandered the streets naked, defecated in public, threw stones at the houses of the pious, preached in gibberish. They have played an enormously important role in Russia.[42] The holy-fool interpretation of Pussy Riot makes sense. Indeed, the members of the group made that connection themselves. But it has some problems. The lives of the holy fools were far more extreme and encompassing than one particular action.

The performance actually feels more rooted in carnival, in festivals like the Feast of Fools. The world is turned upside down. Out-of-place bodies interrupt the status quo and speak as loudly as any words. In the preaching space Pussy Riot's *bodies* become "a visual for justice."[43] The performance invades the liturgical space and brings the sacred down to earth in the profane. The

---

41. Harris, *Carnival*, 139.
42. On holy fools, see Wendy Wright, "Fools for Christ," *Weavings: A Journal of the Christian Spiritual Life* 9 (1994): 23–31; Sergey A. Ivanov, *Holy Fools in Byzantium and Beyond*, trans. Simon Franklin (Oxford: Oxford University Press, 2006); John Saward, *Perfect Fools: Folly for Christ's Sake in Catholic and Orthodox Spirituality* (Oxford: Oxford University Press, 1980); G. P. Fedetov, "The Holy Fools," in *The Religious Mind II: The Middle Ages; The Thirteenth to the Fifteenth Centuries*, ed. John Meyendorff (Cambridge, MA: Harvard University Press, 1966), 316–43; Derek Kruger, *Symeon the Holy Fool: Leontius's Life and the Late Antique City* (Berkeley: University of California Press, 1996). On holy fools in Russia, see Harriet Murav, *Holy Foolishness: Dostoevsky's Novels and the Poetics of Cultural Critique* (Stanford, CA: Stanford University Press, 1992); Ewa M. Thompson, *Understanding Russia: The Holy Fool in Russian Culture* (New York: University Press of America, 1987).
43. Teresa Fry Brown uses this phrase in speaking of the presence of African American women in the pulpits of some churches. See Teresa Fry Brown, "An African American Woman's Perspective: Renovating Sorrow's Kitchen," in *Preaching Justice: Ethic and Cultural Perspectives*, ed. Christine Marie Smith (Cleveland: United Church Press, 1998), 55.

women subvert the ecclesial and political hierarchies. And Mary's "holy defiance" undergirds the entire performance. The Magnificat becomes flesh and dwells among us. In some ways the performance is a kind of mock sermon—a performance from the preaching space that mocks and subverts the patriarch's proclamations supporting Putin.

But there is a deeper reason why the performance is important. Pussy Riot calls the church to be the grotesque Body of Christ. Ecclesiology becomes flesh. The performance calls the church to have more porous boundaries, to become a more leaky body. As Denysenko demonstrates, a central thread running through the performance is exclusion. Protestors—those who opposed Putin's reign—felt excluded from the church. So the women sang, "The head of the KGB, their chief saint, leads protestors to prison under escort." Members of the church had been told they should vote for Putin. "Where does that leave us?" Pussy Riot asked. Feminists were excluded. So they called to Mary, "Become a feminist, become a feminist, become a feminist." LGBTQ+ people were excluded. "Gay-pride sent to Siberia in chains," they sang. And young people, with all their questions and their desire for dialogue and change, felt excluded. Certain bodies were not welcome in the church. So in their carnivalesque performance Pussy Riot invaded the Body of Christ in the name of all these other bodies. They sought to open up Christ's Body, to make it a grotesque body.

Preaching, Homiletics, and the Grotesque Body

Pussy Riot's sermon challenges all of us in the church. I have no interest in critiquing the Russian Orthodox Church. It's not my place or my purpose to do that. I'm interested in the message for preaching and for homiletics and for the Body of Christ. In many ways churches today feel threatened. The old ways are dying, but there is no clarity about the new that is being born. And many of us Christians often seem too concerned about strengthening the body, clarifying the boundaries, centering our identity. Circle the wagons! Maintain orthodoxy! Uphold the tradition! Keep the Body of Christ decent and pure and orderly.

But if we are the *grotesque* Body of Christ there are no closed, static boundaries.[44] That would betray our very identity. Rather, we are open to interruptions, to the stories and memories and persons who unsettle us and subvert our false patterns and our rage for order. For our life lies at the margins of the Body, in our interactions with other bodies, particularly those who have been excluded. Our life and our power become real only when they are drawn out of us by the touch of those who have been considered unclean, outside.

We are the Body of Christ when we become a grotesque, carnivalesque community that defies the world's categories and liberates people from the rankings and norms and prohibitions of the established order. We live as the Body of Christ when we offer an alternative to the weaponized grotesque, so no one is an object, an issue, a thing, but all are welcome and participate together. We serve as the Body of Christ only as we leak and weep and sweat and spit and open our communal Body for the healing of the world.

We live as the Body of Christ, that is, when we are not afraid of change and transition. In our quest for security and stability and certainty, I am concerned that many of us Christians have forgotten that *perpetual transition* is the very character of our life and the church. Dynamic, unsettled change, not static security, is at the heart of our faith. For we live in the interval between the old age that is dying and the new that is being born. As the grotesque Body of Christ, we are always part of an incomplete whole—the carnivalesque reign of a grotesque God. We live in a Body that is mutable and morphing, changed by all our interactions at the boundaries of our life together. We live in the interval between "death and rebirth, insanity and discovery, rubble and revelation." We live as the grotesque Body of Christ, "open, protruding, irregular, secreting, multiple, and changing."

As part of the grotesque Body of Christ, preaching itself is a grotesque practice. That is the case, first of all, because we preach a grotesque gospel. As preachers we continually wrestle with shocking incongruities and perilous paradoxes that disrupt our safe and familiar patterns. We speak of a God "just out of focus, just beyond the reach of language." And we wrestle with this speech not because God is

---

44. See Sigurdson, "Christian Body as a Grotesque Body."

transcendently mysterious, but because the Word became grotesque and dwelt among us. Because we confront a crucified Messiah. The gospel is scandalously beyond the reach of language not because it is so transcendent, but because it is so particular, so fleshy. God-flesh. God-crucified. The scandal of the grotesque and the scandal of particularity go together. Preaching always remains unsettled.

We are like the preacher in Dostoevsky's short story "The Dream of a Ridiculous Man."[45] The man has had a vision of a disturbing gospel, and now he has to preach. But there's a problem. He cannot find the words. "I do not know how to put it into words," he declares. "After my dream I lost the knack of putting things into words. At least, into the most necessary and most important words. But never mind, I shall go on and I shall keep on talking, for I have indeed beheld it with my own eyes, though I cannot describe what I saw."[46] And everyone calls him a madman. Any preacher who deeply engages the grotesque gospel will know that feeling.

But preaching is a grotesque practice for another reason: it is shaped by the dynamic and open life of Jesus' grotesque body. Grotesque preaching calls the church to be open to the world and calls the pulpit to be open to different bodies and new voices. And it calls the preacher to be open as well. For Bakhtin, the rhetorical counterpart to the grotesque body is *dialogue*.[47] In the Body of Christ the truth of preaching will be a dialogical truth, truth that is not the possession of any one person, much less the preacher. Dialogical truth *happens* in encounters with others—just as life happens in the encounter between the porous bodies of Jesus and the bleeding woman.[48] Dialogue is different from vague, open-ended conversation. To have genuine dialogue, all of us speak from where we stand and make some claims from our own perspectives. At the same time, we are also open to interruptions. We are open to truth that happens in

---

45. Fyodor Dostoevsky, "The Dream of a Ridiculous Man: A Fantastic Story," in *The Best Short Stories of Fyodor Dostoevsky*, trans. David Magarshack (New York: Modern Library, 2001), 263–85.
46. Dostoevsky, "Dream of a Ridiculous Man," 284–85.
47. See Marlene Ringgaard Lorensen, *Dialogical Preaching: Bakhtin, Otherness, and Homiletics*, Arbeiten zur Pastoraltheologie, Liturgik und Hymnologie 74 (Göttingen: Vandenhoeck and Ruprecht, 2014).
48. See Carol A. Newsom, "Bakhtin, the Bible, and Dialogic Truth," *Journal of Religion* 76, no. 2 (April 1996): 290–306.

unexpected, even shocking ways. We listen and respond to voices different from our own. And we never seek to use another person's story as mere scaffolding to build our own argument. Truth happens at the edges, in the interchange.[49]

That is why preaching begins with listening. As I have tried to suggest throughout this book, preaching becomes real not only as it engages a grotesque gospel, but also as preachers listen to voices not their own in a kind of polyphonic exchange. Preaching becomes real when truth happens among the cacophony and incongruities of diverse voices and diverse lives. The Word became grotesque and dwelt *among* us. The gospel is not the possession of any of us. The life-giving interchange between Jesus and the bleeding woman happens *between* them, *among* the crowd. It is a dynamic event. The truth of the gospel dwells *among* us. So preachers live in dialogue.

Homiletics lives there too. Homiletics is a grotesque discipline. Speaking metaphorically, I would argue that homiletics can never have a classical body, but is always a grotesque body. Maybe that is why the academy rarely considers it a "classical discipline." Homiletics is "open, protruding, irregular, secreting, multiple, and changing." It is always decentered; it can never close in on itself. Homiletics is an *among* discipline. It exists only *among* many other disciplines; it depends on the connections it makes with biblical studies and theology and history and rhetoric and performance. But that's just the beginning. Homiletics comes *alive* only as it makes these same connections with virtually *everything*. Like the bleeding woman, homiletics lives only as it dares to touch and receive unexpected power from a poem, an inexplicable experience, a popular novel, a punk protest, a photograph, a jazz performance—even from the grotesque. That is the homiletician's fearless, creative, grotesque body of work. It is the shape of homiletical discipleship. For we are servants of the Word. And the Word became grotesque and dwelt among us.

---

49. Conversation with Marlene Ringgaard Lorensen.

Chapter 4

Apocalypse Now

Preaching and the Environmental Grotesque

*I*n her 2018 TED Talk, teenage Swedish environmental activist Greta Thunberg reflected on the time she first heard about "something called climate change or global warming": "I remember thinking," she commented, "that it was very strange that humans, who are an animal species among others, could be capable of changing the Earth's climate. Because if we were, and it was really happening, we wouldn't be talking about anything else."[1]

"We wouldn't be talking about anything else." Her challenge is surely not just to politicians and the media. Though she doesn't mention preachers, Thunberg is challenging us as well. We do a lot of talking. So we need to ask ourselves, Why are *we* talking about anything else in our sermons? Or the better question might be: Why are we so rarely preaching about climate change *at all*?[2] As Thunberg, along with countless others, has noted, we have all the scientific information we need. And the findings become more alarming with every report. Human beings *are* changing the climate because of our addiction to fossil fuels. We face the potential of an "uninhabitable

---

1. Greta Thunberg, "The Disarming Case to Act Right Now on Climate Change," TEDxStockholm, November 2018, https://www.ted.com/talks/greta_thunberg_the_disarming_case_to_act_right_now_on_climate/transcript?language=en#t-24447.

2. I have, for example, *never* heard a sermon preached on climate change in church. Similarly, when I ask my students if they have heard a sermon on global warming, about 10 percent of them raise their hands. Leah Schade has documented the paucity of preaching on climate change. See her *Creation-Crisis Preaching: Ecology, Theology, and Preaching* (St. Louis: Chalice Press, 2015), 1–2.

earth."³ We are in the middle of the sixth mass extinction.⁴ An estimated 140 million to 200 million people will be displaced because of climate stress by 2050.⁵ As a recent U.N. report put it, the situation is "bleak."⁶

The prospects for addressing the problem are equally discouraging. As the Intergovernmental Panel on Climate Change reported in 2018, to keep the temperature rise to 1.5 degrees C and avoid catastrophic consequences, we will need to enact over the next decade unprecedented "transitions in energy, land, urban and infrastructure (including transport and buildings), and industrial systems."⁷ All of that will have to happen against the strong headwinds of corporate and political powers that not only oppose such transitions, but even deny the realities of human-induced climate change itself. It will have to happen at a moment when nationalism, deregulation, and antigovernment sentiment stand in the way of the kind of global cooperation and government involvement that will be essential to avoid catastrophe. Indeed, because of the resistance of the "powers that be," carbon emissions on a global scale have not only not declined, but have continued to increase.⁸ The character Patricia Westerfield, a scientific researcher in David Powers's Pulitzer Prize–winning novel, *The Overstory*, sums up the prospects: "How is extraction ever going to stop? It can't even slow down. The only thing we know how to do is grow. Grow harder; grow faster. More than last year. Growth, all

---

3. See David Wallace-Wells, *The Uninhabitable Earth: Life after Warming* (New York: Tim Dugan Books, 2019).

4. See Elizabeth Kolbert, *The Sixth Extinction: An Unnatural History* (New York: Henry Holt and Company, 2014).

5. A 2018 World Bank study estimated that climate stress would result in 140 million refugees by 2050; the U.N. estimate is 200 million by that date. See Wallace-Wells, *Uninhabitable Earth*, 7. Also Naomi Klein, *On Fire: The (Burning) Case for a Green New Deal* (New York: Simon and Schuster, 2019), 45.

6. "U.N. Environment Programme Emissions Gap Report 2019 Executive Summary," https://wedocs.unep.org/bitstream/handle/20.500.11822/30798/EGR19ESEN.pdf?sequence=13.

7. Intergovernmental Panel on Climate Change, Summary for Policymakers, C.2, https://www.ipcc.ch/sr15/chapter/spm/.

8. See "U.N. Environment Programme Emissions Gap Report 2019 Executive Summary"; also Somini Sengupta, "'Bleak' U.N. Report on a Planet in Peril Looms Over New Climate Talks," *New York Times*, November 26, 2019; https://www.nytimes.com/2019/11/26/climate/greenhouse-gas-emissions-carbon.html. According to the report, greenhouse gas emissions have grown at 1.5 percent per year over the past decade. To avoid the worst effects of climate change, emissions must now decline by 7.6 percent every year between 2020 and 2030.

the way up to the cliff and over. No other possibility."[9] Naomi Klein put the challenge most succinctly in the title of her recent book: *This Changes Everything*.[10] Including preaching.

Apocalypse Now

As people are beginning to recognize, the consequences of climate change are not just in the distant future; they are already upon us. Monster hurricanes and typhoons, catastrophic fires, ravaging rains, and deadly droughts all warn of the creeping reality of global warming. Glaciers are melting, threatening the water supply of millions of people. People are migrating, leaving their homes and cultures to escape from islands that are sinking and drought-stricken areas that will grow no food, only to find inhospitable walls and borders and soldiers keeping them from survival.[11] Insects are dying at alarming rates, portending what some have called an "insect apocalypse" that will threaten food production.[12] At the same time, insects are migrating as temperatures warm, bringing with them deadly diseases to new geographical areas. Plants are blooming too early, confusing the creatures that depend on them and disrupting the farmers who grow them. The sea is lapping into coastal cities and farms, creating flooded streets, killing farmland, and producing miles and miles of ghost forests. And we are already crashing up against the economic challenges of addressing all these cascading calamities simultaneously.[13]

Environmental activist Bill McKibben has argued that we no longer live on *Earth*; we live on a different planet now: *Eaarth*.[14] As he

---

9. David Powers, *The Overstory* (New York: W. W. Norton & Company, 2018), 304.
10. Naomi Klein, *This Changes Everything* (New York: Simon and Schuster, 2014).
11. See, for example, Kirk Semple, "Central American Farmers Head to the U.S., Fleeing Climate Change," *New York Times*, April 13, 2019, https://www.nytimes.com/2019/04/13/world/americas/coffee-climate-change-migration.html.
12. Brooke Jarvis, "The Insect Apocalypse Is Here," *New York Times*, November 27, 2018, https://www.nytimes.com/2018/11/27/magazine/insect-apocalypse.html.
13. Naomi Oreskes and Nicholas Stern, "Climate Change Will Cost Us Even More Than We Think," *New York Times*, October 23, 2019, https://www.nytimes.com/2019/10/23/opinion/climate-change-costs.html; Wallace-Wells, *Uninhabitable Earth*, 115–23.
14. Bill McKibben, *Eaarth: Making Life on a Tough New Planet* (New York: St. Martin's Griffin, 2011).

wrote *in 2011*, "Global warming is no longer a philosophical threat, no longer a future threat, *no longer a threat at all.* It's our reality. We've changed the planet, changed it in large and fundamental ways."[15] A climatologist echoes McKibben's alarm: "Climatologists . . . tend to be a stolid group. We are not given to theatrical rantings about falling skies. . . . Why then are climatologists speaking about the dangers of global warming? The answer is that virtually all of us are now convinced that global warming poses a clear and present danger to civilization."[16]

Heaven and earth and sea are out of sync, unsettled, revolting against the human virus that is infecting them. "Global weirding," some have called it. The cosmos is shaking, stirring up images of apocalypse. Jesus speaks of it:

> But in those days, after that suffering,
>> the sun will be darkened,
>> and the moon will not give its light
>> and the stars will be falling from heaven,
>> and the powers in the heavens will be shaken.
>>> Mark 13:24–25

Then Jesus says something unnerving: Keep alert. Stay awake. Stand at the door and watch. Don't miss it. And warn those who aren't paying attention (vv. 32–37). The entire natural order is out of sync—the sun darkened, the moon not giving its light, stars falling—and Jesus thinks his disciples might miss it! We might not pay attention. We might look the other way. We might not speak up and cry out as faithful doorkeepers.

Jesus was right. The natural order *is* out of sync, but many of us, until recently, have looked the other way. I know I have not paid attention. I have not been a faithful doorkeeper. In all of my writing I have never addressed climate change. I have only recently touched on the environmental crisis in my classes, inadequately preparing my students for the world in which they will be preaching. And I have only preached two sermons on global warming.

I suspect my reasons for ignoring the crisis are not unlike those of many other preachers. I have not stayed alert because I assumed

---

15. McKibben, *Eaarth*, xiii.
16. Quoted in Klein, *This Changes Everything*, 15.

someone else would deal with the problem. The scientists will figure it out. Some new invention will come along. Or maybe we'll get lucky, and the scientists will be wrong.

I have looked the other way because the problem is so overwhelming—and the fossil fuel industry is so powerful. It's demoralizing. What can one person, what can one community do?

I have not paid attention because there are so many compelling concerns. In any given week, a multitude of other issues press in on the sermon. In a culture where the immediate and the spectacular get our attention, the "slow violence" of climate change can be put off till later.[17]

I have not stayed alert because I have the luxury to turn my head: I'm comfortable. There is no immediate need for me to listen to the faithful doorkeepers who are crying, "Watch!" I don't live on those Pacific islands where entire populations are having to relocate because their ancestral home will soon be under water.[18] I don't live in a place where I have to watch glaciers melting, rainfall patterns changing, insects leaving, crops withering, land dying. I don't live in Miami or Houston or Puerto Rico or California or the North Carolina coast where the devastating consequences of climate change are finally waking people up.

Most troubling, I wonder if a cheap and misguided Christian hope has been part of the problem as well. God has promised a new creation, after all—a new heaven and a new earth. The Human One will come in clouds with great power and glory (Mark 13:26). The dire apocalyptic warnings in the Bible, unlike those in much climate fiction, always turn toward hope—hope initiated by an act of God. God will save us. To believe otherwise would surely represent a lack of faith.

Like many people and preachers, I have looked the other way and pretended things will be okay. I have not been a faithful doorkeeper. But now it's time to stop pretending.[19] And now it is very late. The crisis is under way in enormous, almost-impossible-to-prevent ways.

---

17. See Rob Nixon, *Slow Violence and the Environmentalism of the Poor* (Cambridge, MA: Harvard University Press, 2011).

18. See the film about the relocation of the Carteret Islanders, *Sun Come Up*, New Day Films, 2011.

19. See Jonathan Franzen, "What If We Stopped Pretending?" *New Yorker*, September 8, 2019, https://www.newyorker.com/culture/cultural-comment/what-if-we-stopped-pretending.

In the face of potential environmental catastrophe, the grotesque may actually be an invaluable guide.

Preaching and the Environmental Grotesque

Like apocalyptic literature with its disturbing, disruptive imagery, the grotesque shocks us out of our familiar and comfortable patterns. It draws us into a world that is out of sync, creating an unsettled space of unresolved contradictions. We are placed in the "interval of the grotesque," in which the object of our attention remains "just out of focus, just beyond the reach of language."[20] In this "interval" of the grotesque—which I have argued is the interval of the gospel—we live "poised between death and rebirth, insanity and discovery, rubble and revelation."[21]

The grotesque incongruities posed by the enormity and threat of climate change place preachers in a similar interval. We may see the contours and potential catastrophe of global warming, but it remains "just out of focus, just beyond the reach of language." Our old comfortable homiletical patterns and assumptions cease to be adequate, but new ways of preaching have not yet emerged. Preaching, like the planet, finds itself in crisis. In this unsettling environmental interval, a grotesque homiletic may be precisely what we need.[22]

---

20. Geoffrey Galt Harpham, *On the Grotesque: Strategies of Contradiction in Art and Literature* (Princeton, NJ: Princeton University Press, 1982), 3.

21. Harpham, *On the Grotesque*, 18.

22. In this chapter I do not give specific strategies for preaching sermons on climate change, but rather explore the broad contours of such preaching through the lens of the grotesque. Much work has been done on communicating climate change. See, for example, the following resources: Schade, *Creation-Crisis Preaching*; Per Espen Stoknes, "How To Transform Apocalypse Fatigue Into Action on Global Warming," TED Talk, September 2017, https://www.ted.com/talks/per_espen_stoknes_how_to_transform_apocalypse_fatigue _into_action_on_global_warming#t-739; Katharine Hayhoe, "The Most Important Thing You Can Do to Fight Climate Change: Talk about It," TEDWomen, November 2018, https://www .ted.com/talks/katharine_hayhoe_the_most_important_thing_you_can_do_to_fight_climate _change_talk_about_it/transcript?language=en; Center for Research on Environmental Decisions, "The Psychology of Climate Change Communication" (New York: Columbia University, 2009), http://guide.cred.columbia.edu/pdfs/CREDguide_full-res.pdf

Who Knows? Grotesque Hope

Toward the end of her TED Talk, Greta Thunberg makes comments that might disturb Christian preachers:

> Now we're almost at the end of my talk, and this is where people usually start talking about hope: solar panels, wind power, circular economy, and so on, but I'm not going to do that. We've had 30 years of pep-talking and selling positive ideas. And I'm sorry, but it doesn't work. Because if it would have the emissions would have gone down by now. They haven't. And yes, we do need hope, of course we do. But the one thing we need more than hope is action. Once we start to act, hope is everywhere. So instead of looking for hope, look for action. Then, and only then, hope will come.[23]

In a sermon at Riverside Church in New York, Bill McKibben spoke in a similar, though Christian vein. Recognizing that there is absolutely no guarantee that we will win the battle against climate change, and that we have very little time to act, he summons an extremely qualified hope. In church, unlike in the science classroom, he affirms, "We're allowed to believe that if we do all we can . . . then we're allowed to believe that God . . . may still be willing to meet us halfway. Let us pray that is the case, and then let us get to work."[24] *If* we do all we can . . . God *may*. This is hardly the stirring word of hope that preachers so often turn to at the end of sermons.

Both Thunberg and McKibben point preachers to a kind of grotesque hope, possibly the only hope preachers should dare to proclaim in the current context. It is a hope not unlike the grotesque faith discussed in chapter 1. It is a fractured, unresolved hope that involves simultaneously a testimony of hopeful affirmation *and* a testimony of that hope's negation.[25] It is the disturbing, qualified hope proclaimed by the prophet Joel, who with his depictions of environmental catastrophe and an "insect apocalypse" may be the prophet for our time:

---

23. Thunberg, "Disarming Case to Act Right Now on Climate Change."
24. Bill McKibben, "God's Taunt," Riverside Church, New York City, April 28, 2013, https://www.youtube.com/watch?v=geIni_BwjGw. The sermon was preached eight years ago now, and the situation has only grown much more dire.
25. See chapter 1, p. 11.

> Yet even now, says the LORD,
>   return to me with all your heart,
> with fasting, with weeping, and with mourning;
>   rend your hearts and not your clothing.
> Return to the LORD, your God,
>   for he is gracious and merciful,
> slow to anger, and abounding in steadfast love,
>   and relents from punishing.
> Who knows whether he will not turn and relent,
>   and leave a blessing behind him,
> a grain offering and a drink offering
>   for the LORD, your God?
>   *Joel 2:12–14*

Turn from your creation-destroying ways, Joel proclaims. Repent. Act. Do all that you can. God "is gracious and merciful"—"*who knows*," God *may* still be willing to "turn" and "leave a blessing."

God is gracious and merciful. *Who knows?* That is not the kind of hopeful word preachers usually seek at the end of a sermon. Indeed, as Thunberg suggests, the turn to hope is often the ultimate homiletical resolution when everything has been disrupted. As Thunberg says about climate-change talks, so we could say about sermons: "Now we're almost at the end of my [sermon], and this is where we turn to hope." The sermon proclaims the hope that God will resolve things, bring the new creation, and save us. But Thunberg, McKibben, and Joel subvert the pattern of disruption-resolution preaching in the most radical way. They take away our ultimate resolution: an assurance that God will save us. "God is gracious and merciful . . . *who knows?*" The "perilous paradoxicality" of Joel's prophecy frames the homiletical space in which preachers now engage the environmental crisis.[26] Like Thunberg and McKibben, Joel highlights the unresolved character of grotesque hope, simultaneously affirming a testimony of hopeful affirmation *and* a testimony of that hope's negation.

The environmental devastation of climate change, not unlike the cross, is a "catastrophe that interrupts all our neat and settled

---

26. James Luther Adams and William Yates, eds., *The Grotesque in Art and Literature: Theological Reflections* (Grand Rapids: Eerdmans, 1997), xi.

narratives."²⁷ Taking away this comfortable homiletical pattern of disruption-resolution may be precisely what's needed for preaching in the face of the environmental crisis. But without that comforting pattern, preachers may despair. Indeed, it may be our recognition of the environmental grotesque that is silencing preachers. What can we say without the comforting resolution of hopeful assurance?

In the film *First Reformed*, Reverend Toller confronts this reality.²⁸ He finds himself in the interval of the grotesque, and he is not prepared to navigate it except in destructive ways. In the course of the film he confronts the catastrophic future predicted by climate change. And he comes to recognize not only the enormous powers contributing to the problem and resisting all solutions but also the complicity of the church itself with these powers. He is driven into an unresolved, grotesque gospel.

Early in the film, in conversation with a deeply depressed environmental activist, Toller tells the young man that "wisdom is holding two contradictory truths in our mind simultaneously: hope and despair." "Holding these two ideas in our head," he affirms, "is life itself." Following this conversation, Toller reflects in his journal, drawing on Thomas Merton: "I know nothing can change, and I know there is no hope." But "despair is a development of pride so great that it chooses one's certitude rather than admit God is more creative than we are."²⁹ Finally, however, following the suicide of the activist, Toller is left with the question the young man posed to him: "Will God forgive us for what we are doing to his creation?" Toller is left with Joel's "Who knows?" Unable to sustain that unresolved tension, he descends down a horrifically destructive path.

In an interview, the director of the film, Paul Schrader, was asked about this question: "Toller's relationship with young environmentalists leads him to an agonizing question: Can God forgive us?" And Schrader responds with a disturbing reply: "I have a secular answer, but it's not the correct answer. If the question is 'can God forgive

---

27. Richard Lischer, "The Limits of Story," *Interpretation* 38 (January 1984): 33.
28. *First Reformed*, directed by Paul Schrader, 2018, A24 Films.
29. For a helpful book that explores a kind of hope consistent with this comment, see Rebecca Solnit, *Hope in the Dark: Untold Histories, Wild Possibilities*, 3rd ed. (Chicago: Haymarket Books, 2016).

us,' the secular answer is he has to; that's why we made him. That's his job."³⁰

Too often preachers follow this "secular answer," rather than Joel's unsettling witness to the living God. Schrader rather shockingly invites preachers to beware of our neat, comfortable patterns, which God interrupted in the crucifixion and which may be interrupted again in the current environmental context. We serve the living God, not a god of our creation who must forgive us and save humanity. As Joel proclaims of the living God, "Who knows?"

In the context of climate change, hope cannot serve as the nice, neat resolution for Christian preaching. Hope will remain an unresolved resolution. In the grotesque environmental interval "poised between death and rebirth, insanity and discovery, rubble and revelation," we preach simultaneously a testimony of hopeful affirmation *and* a testimony of that hope's negation. Otherwise hope becomes dangerous, lessening the urgency of the moment and even leading to inaction. And inaction may result in negating the very hope we proclaim by leading to environmental and civilizational catastrophe. There is no room now for cheap hope, just as Dietrich Bonhoeffer decried "cheap grace."³¹ Only along the path of faithful action that does all it can to address the environmental crisis do we dare proclaim hope—and only then with Joel's caveat: "Who knows?"

This approach to hope will mean giving up neat homiletical patterns that move simplistically from disruption to the ultimate resolution of hope. It will mean living in the grotesque interval of unresolved contradictions between the old and the new age. It will mean risking the familiar anathema of works righteousness by affirming that action and hope are inseparable—that hope "is not a thing you *feel* / but something you *do*."³² The current crisis, like the

---

30. A. O. Scott, "'First Reformed' Asks, Can God Forgive Us? Its Director Has an Answer," *New York Times*, June 20, 2018, https://www.nytimes.com/2018/06/20/movies/first-reformed-paul-schrader.html.

31. Dietrich Bonhoeffer, *The Cost of Discipleship*, rev. ed., trans. R. H. Fuller (New York: Macmillan, 1963), 45–60. In *The Overstory*, David Powers turns our assumptions about hope on their head. One of his characters comments about radical, environmental activists, "Hopelessness makes them determined. Nothing's more beautiful than that" (304).

32. Nickole Brown, "Against Despair: The Kid Goat," in *To Those Who Were Our First Gods* (Studio City, CA: Rattle, 2018), 36.

gospel itself, challenges our comfortable patterns and calls forth radical and possibly disturbing new approaches to preaching.

Climate change suggests the need for a polyphonic approach to hope in sermons.[33] A polyphonic approach incorporates a variety of different voices that remain in tension without being subsumed into the "authorial voice" of the preacher. Joel's prophecy itself reflects the tensiveness of such polyphonic preaching. He speaks an extreme word of judgment, which in fact takes the form of environmental devastation—an "insect apocalypse" accompanied by catastrophic warfare (1:1–2:11). He also speaks an extreme word of hope, unqualified at times by any human initiative (2:18–27). Simultaneously, however, he links any blessing of God to radical repentance and decisive new action (2:12–17). But even with repentance, as I've noted, Joel can only say of God's blessing, "Who knows?" (2:14). Joel's extreme, polyphonic prophecy represents the unresolved incongruities of the grotesque with which preachers will need to grapple in the midst of climate change. While such polyphonic preaching may seem frustrating to preachers who desire a clear, hopeful resolution in their sermons, the enormity of the catastrophe creates a grotesque space that prevents any single response—a space that calls forth an unsettled, grotesque hope.

Environmental Justice: Resisting the Weaponized Grotesque

As I noted earlier, in the unsettled space of the grotesque, a great temptation is to shore up boundaries, build walls, and circle wagons. Naomi Klein notes, "Climate change isn't just about things getting hotter and wetter: under our current economic and political order, it's about things getting meaner and uglier."[34] One of the ugliest expressions of this tendency is the weaponization of the grotesque, the use

---

33. Mikhail Bakhtin, with his emphasis on dialogical truth (see chapter 3) explores the polyphonic novel, which he finds exemplified in the works of Dostoevsky. See Mikhail Bakhtin, *Problems of Dostoevsky's Poetics*, trans. Caryl Emerson, Theory and History of Literature 8 (Minneapolis: University of Minnesota Press, 1984). For an application of Bakhtin's theories to preaching, see Marlene Lorensen, *Dialogical Preaching: Bakhtin, Otherness, and Homiletics*, Arbeiten zur Pastoraltheologie, Liturgik und Hymnologie 74 (Göttingen: Vandenhoeck and Ruprecht, 2013).

34. Klein, *On Fire*, 166.

of the grotesque to turn humans into animals or things that need to be excluded or exterminated. The unsettled, grotesque realities of climate change exacerbate this tendency and invite the use of the weaponized grotesque on an unprecedented scale. Preachers will be challenged to resist the ways the weaponized grotesque will be employed (is already being employed) to justify policies that serve more powerful populations and sacrifice those people most vulnerable to the ravages of climate change.

In *The Christian Imagination* Willie Jennings highlights the connection between displacement from land and the dehumanization of people. When white Europeans removed African people from their land, he argues, they uncoupled identities from both time and place and enabled slaves to be signified solely by "race." Whiteness "replaced the earth as the signifier of identities."[35] "The central effect of the loss of the earth as an identity signifier," Jennings writes, "was that native identities, tribal, communal, familial, and spatial, were constricted to simply their bodies, leaving behind the very ground that enables and facilitates the articulation of identity."[36] Displacement from the land thus lay at the root of the invention of race. It was an initial step in dehumanizing a population. Separating people from their land created a context in which white oppressors could weaponize the grotesque, equate humanity with whiteness, and signify a population as less than human. The relationship between displacement from land and the weaponized grotesque has deep roots.

This dynamic relationship between displacement and dehumanization continues. The climate crisis, created by colonial powers, is displacing poor people and people of color—people who have contributed virtually nothing to the crisis—from their land. And the weaponized grotesque, used to dehumanize entire populations and cultures, continues to justify these developments and to salve the consciences of those in power.

In her classic essay "The Greater Common Good," Booker Prize–winning author Arundhati Roy analyzes this process as she examines the construction of mega-dams in India.[37] The essay begins with a

---

35. Willie James Jennings, *The Christian Imagination: Theology and the Origins of Race* (New Haven, CT: Yale University Press, 2010), 58; see also 39.
36. Jennings, *Christian Imagination*, 43.
37. Arundhati Roy, "The Greater Common Good," in *The Cost of Living* (New York: Modern Library, 1999), 1–90.

laugh. "I stood on a hill and laughed out loud," Roy writes in her opening sentence. From that hill Roy views the homes and fields and forests of tribal hamlets "ranged across the crowns of low, bald hills." She watches "little children with their littler goats scuttling across the landscape like motorized peanuts." And she knows that the entire area will soon be drowned and the people displaced as the monsoon waters rise behind a mega-dam to submerge the land. With that displacement, a "civilization older than Hinduism" will be destroyed and human identities rooted in the land will be wrecked. Roy also knows that the human communities she sees will be dehumanized to justify their displacement in the name of "progress" and "the greater common good." Aware of all that, she senses the absurd claims (and lies) of those in power who have assured her that the children will have wonderful places to play in their resettlement colonies. So she laughs at the absurdity of it all.[38]

Roy's laughter interrupts the process of dehumanization. It is laughter that attends deeply to the grotesque incongruity of human lives being treated as disposable objects on a massive scale. Throughout the remainder of the article, Roy schools her readers in the rhetoric of interruption. She exposes the large-scale bureaucratic use of the weaponized grotesque, and she counters that with the courageous and tragic stories of its victims.[39] Indeed, she reveals that the weaponized grotesque is necessary to make human populations disappear from the imagination so that they can be displaced and left to suffer and die. Before the literal displacement of peoples occurs, they have to be "imaginatively displaced" by rhetoric that makes entire communities invisible. Before their literal evacuation, they become "unimagined communities."[40] The consequence is hundreds of thousands of environmental refugees. In the face of this dehumanizing, rhetorical use of the weaponized grotesque, Roy shifts our point of view and invites us to imagine the dams

> not just from the distant orbit of the powerful modernizers (those who, in her words, conduct "imperialism by email") but from

---

38. Roy, "Greater Common Good," 7–8.
39. Roy herself does not use the phrase "weaponized grotesque," though she powerfully describes the reality.
40. See Nixon, *Slow Violence*, 150, 152. I am indebted to Nixon's insightful interpretation of Roy's essay.

the more intimate orbit of the powerless as well, that is, from the vantage point of those whom we might variously call modernity's surplus people, its developmental refugees, and its virtual uninhabitants.[41]

In exposing the weaponized grotesque, Roy highlights the large-scale bureaucratic use of this rhetoric that we can anticipate as climate change forces the displacement of entire populations—and, indeed, civilizations. This rhetoric is embedded in the genre of the report, which veils the weaponized grotesque that is actually operative.[42] Statistics, acronyms, and euphemisms all serve to dehumanize populations. Human beings are reduced to numbers on a spreadsheet, without human faces or stories. Or even more profoundly, people are not just reduced to statistics. Often no official figures of casualties are even kept. (Figures, for example, were not kept of children separated from their parents at the U.S. southern border.) Then people are reduced to "non-statistics, a whole different level of dehumanization."[43] As preachers, we should beware of statistics—including statistics we are often tempted to use in our sermons. They can be vehicles of the weaponized grotesque. We should especially pay attention to the failure of bureaucracies to provide casualty figures at all. Such rhetoric turns peoples into "uninhabitants."[44]

And we should keep an eye out for acronyms. These also dehumanize people and justify their displacement. In Roy's article, the children playing with their goats, along with all the others living in the hamlets, become PAPS, "Project-Affected People." Roy writes, "They help, these acronyms, they manage to mutate muscle and blood into cold statistics. PAPS soon cease to be people."[45] Human beings are concealed behind a "bloodless, technocratic, deviously neutral term [that] obscures the fact that those affected are inevitably negatively affected—often doomed—by the project in question."[46] Similarly, euphemisms like "submergence zones," which designate an area to be flooded, not only obscure the human beings who live

---

41. Nixon, *Slow Violence*, 159–60.
42. Nixon, *Slow Violence*, 168.
43. Nixon, *Slow Violence*, 162.
44. Nixon, *Slow Violence*, 152.
45. Roy, "Greater Common Good," 32.
46. Nixon, *Slow Violence*, 163.

there, but turn the rhythms and flora and fauna of the land, with their profound role in the humanity of those who live there, into a singular zone—a thing that can be impassionately and abstractly dismissed in a report.

Throughout her essay Roy counters this dehumanizing rhetoric that turns human beings into calculatedly overgeneralized statistics, acronyms, and euphemisms.[47] In her counter-rhetoric, Roy embodies and calls for writers—and preachers!—"who can translate cash-flow charts and scintillating boardroom speeches into real stories about real people with real lives. Stories about what it's like to lose your home, your land, your job, your dignity, your past, and your future to an invisible force. To someone or something you can't see. You can't hate. You can't even imagine."[48] She calls for an art "committed to undoing verbally and bureaucratically inflicted absence":[49] "An art which can make the impalpable palpable, make the intangible tangible, and the invisible visible. An art which can draw out the incorporeal adversary and make it real."[50] Confronting the massive displacements that will come with climate change, preachers too will be called to develop a rhetoric that resists the weaponized grotesque and engages "real stories about real people with real lives."

In an essay titled "Let Them Drown: The Violence of Othering in a Warming World," Naomi Klein unmasks the same dynamic occurring globally that Roy exposes in India.[51] Drawing on Edward Said's concept of "othering," Klein notes the ways in which both fossil fuel extraction and the consequences of climate change require othering, which involves "disregarding, essentializing, denuding the humanity of another culture, people, or geographical region."[52] It is, in the terms I have been using, a means of employing the weaponized grotesque.

---

47. Nixon, *Slow Violence*, 170.
48. Arundhati Roy, "The Ladies Have Feelings, So . . . Shall We Leave It to the Experts?" in *Power Politics* (Cambridge, MA: South End Press, 2001), 32.
49. Nixon, *Slow Violence*, 170.
50. Roy, "Ladies Have Feelings," 32.
51. In Klein, *On Fire*, 149–68. For another exploration of the intersectionality of environmental injustice, particularly the impact on poor people, people of color, and women of color, see Melanie L. Harris, *Ecowomanism: African American Women and Earth-Honoring Faiths* (Maryknoll, NY: Orbis Books, 2017).
52. Edward Said, *Orientalism* (New York: Pantheon Books, 1978) quoted in Klein, *On Fire*, 155.

As with the "submergence zones" in India, the fossil fuel industry has required "national sacrifice areas," where people and places could both be sacrificed to the demand for fossil fuels. Dehumanization, Klein demonstrates, has necessarily accompanied fossil fuel extraction. The tar sands of Alberta, Canada. Mountaintop removal in Appalachia. Oil wells in the Niger Delta in Africa, "poisoned with an Exxon Valdez worth of spilled oil every year." Urban neighborhoods that bear the brunt of toxic waste. In these and countless other areas, human beings and their land and culture have been euphemized into "sacrifice zones." The fossil fuel industry, creating such "sacrificial people and places," has engaged in a bureaucratic, corporate form of the weaponized grotesque for a long time.[53]

This kind of dehumanization now continues on a massive scale as the earth warms. The sacrifice zones required by fossil fuel extraction are expanding because of the warming caused by that very extraction. The same racist use of the weaponized grotesque discussed in chapter 2 can be seen on a global scale in response to the consequences of climate change. Indeed, the refusal by wealthy countries to lower emissions even in the face of clear scientific evidence of the dangers has required a kind of implicit weaponized grotesque. This kind of recklessness "would have been impossible without institutional racism . . . without all the potent tools on offer that allow the powerful to discount the lives of the less powerful."[54] Even the frequently cited goal of limiting warming to 2.0 degrees C (3.6 degrees F), which has been "defined as a strategy for averting 'dangerous' levels of warming," contains within it an implicit discounting of people of color. As Klein writes,

> But the temperature target—pushed by wealthy nations in Europe and North America—would likely not be enough to save some low-lying small island states from annihilation. And in Africa, where drought linked to climate change was at that time menacing

---

53. Klein, *On Fire*, 156–57. Klein also critiques a form of "green colonialism" through which corporations, under the guise of environmental engagement, dehumanize and displace peoples and cultures. She cites, in particular, the land grabbing that takes place as corporations seek "carbon offsets" by buying up large tracts of forests that displace indigenous people (152). Under the guise of environmental concern, the weaponized grotesque operates to further environmental injustice.

54. Klein, *On Fire*, 155.

many lives in the eastern part of the continent, the target would translate into a full-scale humanitarian disaster. Clearly the definition of "dangerous" climate change had more than a little to do with the wildly unequal ways in which human lives are counted.[55]

African delegates at the U.N. climate summit in Copenhagen called the 2-degree goal a "death sentence."[56]

When the stress of climate change creates refugees of people of color, powerful nations resort to the weaponized grotesque by referring to them as a "flood" or an "infestation" that threatens national identities. People displaced by raging storms and rising seas and devastating droughts are themselves cruelly and ironically depicted as natural disasters. This rhetorical dehumanization of refugees simply makes explicit the bureaucratic weaponized grotesque that has dehumanized them and their cultures before they were even forced to leave their lands. Indeed, climate change refugees actually endure the deepest form of dehumanization; they are not even currently recognized under international law. Like many of the persons displaced by mega-dams in India, they truly become "non-inhabitants."

Pointing beyond India's mega-dams to the larger forces shaping climate change and environmental injustice, Arundhati Roy writes that globalization is "like a light which shines brighter and brighter on a few people and the rest are in darkness, wiped out. They simply can't be seen. Once you get used to not seeing something, then, slowly, it's no longer possible to see it."[57] Beneath all the environmental talk of mitigation and adaptation, preachers will be called to address the dehumanization that propels policy on climate change—often in the name of the "greater common good" defined by those in power. Preachers will be challenged to reject the "sacrifice zone mentality" that is applied to people and places.[58] Affirming the humanity and value of all people, preachers will be called to denounce the meanness and ugliness of the weaponized grotesque

---

55. Naomi Klein, "Why #BlackLivesMatter Should Transform the Climate Debate," *The Nation*, December 12, 2014, https://www.thenation.com/article/what-does-blacklivesmatter-have-do-climate-change/.
56. Klein, *On Fire*, 165. The current goal is 1.5 degrees. See above, p. 60.
57. Quoted in Nixon, *Slow Violence*, 172.
58. Klein, *On Fire*, 167.

that consigns entire cultures to displacement and even extinction. We will be called to help people "see."

Back to the Grotto: The Environmental Grotesque Body

In chapter 3 I argued that the grotesque body decenters persons. The grotesque body is dynamic, open, and changing; it is a forever-unfinished body that lives at the margins of the body as it interacts with other bodies. It does not have clear and rigid boundaries. The grotesque body is not self-contained, finished, or individual. It is an inescapably social body, a transgressive body, crossing boundaries in a generative process of death and renewal. Jesus' body is likewise a grotesque body. The boundaries of his body are never closed or static, but open to humanity. Throughout the Gospels, from his ministry through the crucifixion and resurrection, Jesus' body is a porous, leaky, transgressive body through which the weak power of God moves to save. The Word became grotesque and dwelt among us.

The grotesque body, however, not only decenters the individual person; it also decenters the human. The grotesque body is an *environmental* body because it is intertwined not only with other human bodies, but with the earth, with animals, with things. As Mikhail Bakhtin writes, "The unfinished and open body (dying, bringing forth and being born) is not separated from the world by clearly defined boundaries; it is blended with the world, with animals, with objects. It is cosmic, it represents the entire material bodily world in all its elements."[59] Or as the great environmentalist John Muir put it, "When we try to pick out anything by itself, we find it hitched to everything else in the universe."[60]

The grotesque body in this broad sense challenges a human-centered homiletic, which has narrowed preachers' focus to human concerns and contributed to the exploitation of the earth. In our current context, we need to return to the grotto and the original drawings that were interpreted as grotesque. Those drawings were viewed as grotesque because, from a particular human viewpoint,

---

59. Mikhail Bakhtin, *Rabelais and His World*, trans. Helene Iswolsky (Bloomington: Indiana University Press, 1984), 27.
60. Quoted in Elizabeth A. Johnson, *Creation and the Cross: The Mercy of God for a Planet in Peril* (Maryknoll, NY: Orbis Books, 2018), 159.

they represented a mixing of entities that should not be combined. Elements of humans, animals, plants, and beasts were exuberantly combined into seemingly incongruous figures. The strange drawings, however, reflect an understanding of the natural world that is more profound than the humanistic perspective of those interpreters who defined them as grotesque. Their shocking interruption of a human-centric world may be precisely the challenge homiletics needs today.

The seemingly wild and incongruous images in the grottos are now affirmed in contemporary scientific insights. As the character Patricia Westerfield notes in *The Overstory*, "You and the tree in your backyard come from a common ancestor. A billion and a half years ago, the two of you parted ways. But even now, after an immense journey in separate directions, that tree and you still share a quarter of your genes."[61] Theologian Elizabeth Johnson further expands this vision:

> Human beings are part of an interconnected whole. Scientific knowledge today is repositioning the human species as an intrinsic part of the evolutionary network of life on planet Earth, which in turn is a part of the solar system, which itself formed out of the dust and gas of ancient exploding stars. The landscape of our imagination expands when we realize that human connection to nature is so deep that we can no longer completely define human identity without including the great sweep of cosmic development and our shared biological ancestry with all organisms in the community of life.[62]

The images in the grotto gesture toward this interconnectedness of humans with every organism in creation.

Johnson takes this insight in a challenging theological direction through her work on "deep incarnation," which invites us to "rethink the scope and significance of incarnation in an ecological direction."[63] She begins where I began in chapter 3, with John 1:14, though she

---

61. Powers, *Overstory*, 132.
62. Johnson, *Creation and the Cross*, 184.
63. Johnson, *Creation and Cross*, 158–94. The phrase was coined by Danish theologian Neils Henrik Gregersen. See his article "The Cross of Christ in an Evolutionary World," *Dialog* 40, no. 3 (2001): 192–207.

dramatically expands the Gospel's affirmation: "The Word became flesh and dwelt among us." Theologically, Johnson affirms that Jesus' fleshy body is a cosmic body. According to Johnson, the term "flesh" never simply signifies human beings in Scripture. Rather, it refers to the entire "natural sphere of what is fragile, vulnerable, perishable," and it echoes God's covenants with all of creation going back to Noah (Gen. 9:15–17).[64] In becoming flesh, that is, Jesus takes into himself, not just humanity, but the entire created order. "The flesh that the Word became as a particular human being is part of the tree of evolving life on earth, which in turn is part of the vast body of the cosmos."[65] "Think of it this way," Johnson writes:

> As a creature of earth, Jesus was a complex living unit of minerals and fluids, an item in the carbon, oxygen, and nitrogen cycles. The atoms comprising his body were once part of other creatures. The genetic structure of the cells in his body were kin to the flowers, fish, frogs, finches, foxes, the whole community of life that descended from common ancestors in the ancient seas.[66]

Jesus can thus be called in Colossians, "the firstborn of all creation," in whom "all things in heaven and on earth were created" (1:15–16).

As Johnson articulates, Jesus' grotesque body is far more expansive than the leaky body I discussed in chapter 3. Jesus' body actually welcomes into itself the entire cosmos, not just human beings. Jesus lives in solidarity with all creatures; he accompanies all of creation in his life, death, and resurrection.[67] Jesus' grotesque body decenters the human, reminding us that redemption is not simply a human concern, but encompasses all creatures, the entire cosmos. Jesus' crucified, grotesque body suffers the consequences of environmental catastrophe along with the earth. And his resurrected body likewise holds promise for all of creation. The grotesque interval between crucifixion and resurrection, reflected in the San Salvador chapel, echoes in the groaning of the earth itself. The chapel's gruesome stations of the cross, at which the preacher looks as she preaches, morph into images of catastrophic, environmental devastation.

---

64. Johnson, *Creation and Cross*, 184.
65. Johnson, *Creation and Cross*, 184.
66. Johnson, *Creation and Cross*, 185–86.
67. Johnson, *Creation and Cross*, 189.

In the grotesque Body of Christ Christians are deeply and inextricably interwoven with the cosmos. We cannot treat creation as a commodity to exploit; to do so is to commodify Jesus himself. Rather, we accompany the earth, we live in solidarity with creation, at a depth that ends our silence.[68] Preaching Jesus now calls us to speak not just for human beings, but for the entire created order embodied in his incarnation. No Christ-centered sermon can avoid that. For many preachers this new perspective will be unsettling and disorienting; it will require new homiletical language and patterns and forms.[69] But who knows? Formed by sermons "poised between death and rebirth, insanity and discovery, rubble and revelation," the grotesque Body of Christ may begin to live into "the potentiality of another world, another order, another way of life."[70]

---

68. Johnson, *Creation and Cross*, 159.
69. On the need for new language, patterns, and forms, see Lidia Yuknavitch's postapocalyptic novel, *The Book of Joan* (New York: HarperCollins, 2017), 257.
70. Bakhtin, *Rabelais and His World*, 230.

Selected Bibliography

Adams, James Luther, and Wilson Yates, eds. *The Grotesque in Art and Literature: Theological Reflections.* Grand Rapids: Eerdmans, 1997.
Akhmatova, Anna. *Requiem.* In *The Complete Poems of Anna Akhmatova*, translated by Judith Hemschemeyer, edited by Roberta Reeder, 95. Somerville, MA: Zephyr Press, 1990.
Alexander, Michelle. *The New Jim Crow: Mass Incarceration in the Age of Colorblindness.* New York: New Press, 2010.
Bakhtin, Mikhail. *Problems of Dostoevsky's Poetics.* Theory and History of Literature 8, edited and translated by Caryl Emerson. Minneapolis: University of Minnesota Press, 1984.
———. *Rabelais and His World.* Translated by Helene Iswolsky. Bloomington: Indiana University Press, 1984.
Baldwin, James. "Everybody's Protest Novel." In *Notes of a Native Son*, 13–23. Boston: Beacon Press, 1955.
Beal, Timothy. "Pussy Riot's Theology." *Chronicle of Higher Education*, September 17, 2012, https://www.chronicle.com/article/Pussy-Riots-Theology/134398.
Beecher, Henry Ward. *Yale Lectures on Preaching.* 3 volumes. New York: Fords, Howard, and Hulbert, 1892.
Blackmon, Douglas. *Slavery by Another Name: The Re-Enslavement of Black Americans from the Civil War to World War II.* New York: Anchor Press, 2008.
Bowler, Kate. *Everything Happens for a Reason and Other Lies I've Loved.* New York: Random House, 2018.
Brooks, Phillips. *On Preaching.* New York: Seabury Press, 1964.
Brown, Alexandra R. *The Cross and Human Transformation: Paul's Apocalyptic Word in 1 Corinthians.* Minneapolis: Fortress Press, 1995.
Brown, Teresa Fry. "An African American Woman's Perspective: Renovating Sorrow's Kitchen." In *Preaching Justice: Ethic and Cultural Perspectives*, edited by Christine Marie Smith, 43–61. Cleveland: United Church Press, 1998.
Bussie, Jacqueline. *The Laughter of the Oppressed: Ethical and Theological Resistance in Wiesel, Morrison, and Endo.* New York: T & T Clark, 2007.
Cassuto, Leonard. *The Inhuman Race: The Racial Grotesque in American Literature and Culture.* New York: Columbia University Press, 1997.
Cliff, Brian. *Irish Crime Fiction.* London: Palgrave Macmillan, 2018.
Clifton, Lucille. "why some people be mad at me sometime." In *Blessing the Boats: New and Selected Poems, 1998–2000*, 38. Rochester, NY: BOA Editions, 2000.
Colón-Emeric, Edgardo. *Óscar Romero's Theological Vision: Liberation and the*

Transfiguration of the Poor. South Bend, IN: University of Notre Dame Press, 2018.

Cone, James H. *The Cross and the Lynching Tree*. Maryknoll, NY: Orbis Books, 2011.

Davis, D. Diane. *Breaking Up [at] Totality: A Rhetoric of Laughter*. Carbondale: Southern Illinois University Press, 2000.

Davis, Natalie Zemon. "Women on Top." In *Society and Culture in Early Modern France*, 124–51. Stanford, CA: Stanford University Press, 1975.

Denysenko, Nicholas. "An Appeal to Mary: An Analysis of Pussy Riot's Punk Performance in Moscow." *Journal of the American Academy of Religion* 81, no. 4 (December 2013): 1061–92.

Dietschy, Nathalie. "From Urine to the Hammer: Andres Serrano and the Stigmata of Scandal." In *Andres Serrano: Uncensored Photographs*, 34–41. Brussels: Royal Museums of Fine Arts of Belgium, 2016.

Di Renzo, Anthony. *American Gargoyles: Flannery O'Connor and the Medieval Grotesque*. Carbondale: Southern Illinois University Press, 1993.

Dostoevsky, Fyodor. "The Dream of a Ridiculous Man: A Fantastic Story." In *The Best Short Stories of Fyodor Dostoevsky*, translated by David Magarshack, 263–85. New York: Modern Library, 2001.

Duvall, Severn. "Uncle Tom's Cabin: The Sinister Side of the Patriarchy." *New England Quarterly* 36, no. 1 (March 1963): 3–22.

Edwards, Justin D., and Rune Graulund. *Grotesque*. New Critical Idiom. London: Routledge, 2013.

Ekman, Kerstin. *Blackwater*. Translated by Joan Tate. New York: Picador, 1993.

Endo, Shusaku. *Silence*. Translated by William Johnston. New York: Taplinger, 1980.

Feminist Press. *Pussy Riot! A Punk Prayer for Freedom*. New York: Feminist Press, 2013.

A Film about Anna Akhmatova. New York: Das Films, TurnstyleTV, 2008.

First Reformed. Directed by Paul Schrader. A24 Films, 2018.

Gates, Henry Louis, Jr. "Introduction to *The Annotated Uncle Tom's Cabin*." In *The Annotated Uncle Tom's Cabin*, edited by Henry Louis Gates Jr. and Hollis Robbins, xi–xxx. New York: W. W. Norton, 2007.

Gessen, Masha. *Words Will Break Cement: The Passion of Pussy Riot*. New York: Riverhead Books, 2014.

Goodwin, James. *Modern American Grotesque: Literature and Photography*. Columbus: Ohio State University Press, 2009.

Harpham, Geoffrey. "The Grotesque: First Principles." *Journal of Aesthetics and Art Criticism* 34, no. 4 (1976): 461–68.

———. *On the Grotesque: Strategies of Contradiction in Art and Literature*. Princeton, NJ: Princeton University Press, 1982.

Harris, Max. *Carnival and Other Christian Festivals: Folk Theology and Folk Performance*. Austin: University of Texas Press, 2003.

Harris, Melanie L. *Ecowomanism: African American Women and Earth-Honoring Faiths*. Maryknoll, NY: Orbis Books, 2017.

Selected Bibliography 83

Harrisville, Roy A. *Fracture: The Cross as Irreconcilable in the Language and Thought of the Biblical Writers.* Grand Rapids: Eerdmans, 2006.
Hedrick, Joan D. *Harriet Beecher Stowe: A Life.* New York: Oxford University Press, 1994.
Hyde, Lewis. *Trickster Makes This World: Mischief, Myth, and Art.* New York: North Point Press, 1998.
Jennings, Willie James. *The Christian Imagination: Theology and the Origins of Race.* New Haven, CT: Yale University Press, 2010.
Johnson, Elizabeth A. *Creation and the Cross: The Mercy of God for a Planet in Peril.* Maryknoll, NY: Orbis Books, 2018.
Jones, Malcolm. "The Parodic Sermon in Medieval and Early Modern England." *Medium Aevum* 66, no. 1 (1997): 90–114.
Kayser, Wolfgang. *The Grotesque in Art and Literature.* Translated by Ulrich Weisstein. Bloomington: Indiana University Press, 1963.
Kelley, Mary. *Private Woman, Public Stage: Literary Domesticity in Nineteenth-Century America.* 1984; reprint, Chapel Hill: University of North Carolina Press, 2002.
Klein, Naomi. *On Fire: The (Burning) Case for a Green New Deal.* New York: Simon and Schuster, 2019.
———. *This Changes Everything: Capitalism vs. the Climate.* New York: Simon and Schuster, 2014.
———. "Why #BlackLivesMatter Should Transform the Climate Debate." *The Nation*, December 12, 2014, https://www.thenation.com/article/what-does-blacklivesmatter-have-do-climate-change/.
Kolbert, Elizabeth. *The Sixth Extinction: An Unnatural History.* New York: Henry Holt and Company, 2014.
Krinks, Andrew. "Why It Pays to Imprison: Unmasking the Prison-Industrial Complex." In *And the Criminals with Him: Essays in Honor of Will D. Campbell and All the Reconciled*, edited by Will D. Campbell and Richard C. Goode, 54–69. Eugene, OR: Cascade Press, 2012.
Kuryluk, Ewa. *Salome and Judas in the Cave of Sex: The Grotesque; Origins, Iconography, Techniques.* Evanston, IL: Northwestern University Press, 1987.
Lemire, Elise. *"Miscegenation": Making Race in America.* Philadelphia: University of Pennsylvania Press, 2002.
Lippard, Lucy R. "Andres Serrano: The Spirit and the Letter." *Art in America* 78 (April 1990): 238–45.
Lischer, Richard. "The Limits of Story." *Interpretation* 38 (January 1984): 26–38.
Lorensen, Marlene Ringgaard. *Dialogical Preaching: Bakhtin, Otherness, and Homiletics.* Arbeiten zur Pastoraltheologie, Liturgik und Hymnologie 74. Göttingen: Vandenhoeck and Ruprecht, 2013.
Martinez, Demetria. "Upon Waking." In *The Devil's Workshop*, 31. Tucson: University of Arizona Press, 2002.
McCracken, David. *The Scandal of the Gospels: Jesus, Story, and Offense.* New York: Oxford University Press, 1994.

McCray, Donyelle. "Sweating, Spitting, and Cursing: Intimations of the Sacred." *Practical Matters* 9 (April 2015): 62–72.
McKibben, Bill. *Eaarth: Making Life on a Tough New Planet*. New York: St. Martin's Griffin, 2011.
———. "God's Taunt." Riverside Church, New York City, April 28, 2013, https://www.youtube.com/watch?v=geIni_BwjGw.
Meggit, Justin. "Laughing and Dreaming at the Foot of the Cross: Context and Reception of a Religious Symbol?" In *Modern Spiritualities: An Inquiry*, edited by Laurence Brown, Bernard C. Farr, and R. Joseph Hoffmann, 63–70. Amherst, MA: Prometheus Books, 1997.
Metzler, Jessica. "Lusty Ape-Men and Imperiled White Womanhood: Reading Race in a 1930s Poe Film Adaptation." In *Adapting Poe: Re-Imaginings in Popular Culture*, edited by Carl H. Sederholm, 31–43. Palgrave Macmillan, 2012.
Morrison, Toni. *The Bluest Eye*. New York: Vintage International, 2007.
Moss, Candida. "The Man with the Flow of Power: Porous Bodies in Mark 5:25–34." *Journal of Biblical Literature* 129, no. 3 (2010): 507–19.
Muir, Edward. "Carnival and the Lower Body." In *Ritual in Early Modern Europe*, 85–116. Cambridge, MA: Cambridge University Press, 1997.
Newsom, Carol A. "Bakhtin, the Bible, and Dialogic Truth." *Journal of Religion* 76, no. 2 (April 1996): 290–306.
Nixon, Rob. *Slow Violence and the Environmentalism of the Poor*. Cambridge, MA: Harvard University Press, 2011.
O'Connell, Michael. "Mockery, Farce, and *Risus Paschalis* in the York *Christ before Herod*." In *Farce and Farcical Elements*. Ludus: Medieval and Early Renaissance Theatre and Drama 6, edited by Wim Husken, 45–58. Amsterdam: Rodopi, 2002.
O'Connor, Flannery. "Some Aspects of the Grotesque in Southern Fiction." In *Mystery and Manners: Occasional Prose*, edited by Sally and Robert Fitzgerald, 36–50. New York: Farrar, Strauss and Giroux, 1969.
Orr, Gregory. *The Blessing: A Memoir*. San Francisco: Council Oaks Books, 2002.
Parsons, Ben, and Bas Jongenelen. "'The Sermon on Saint Nobody': A Verse Translation of a Middle Dutch Parodic Sermon." *Journal of American Folklore* 123, no. 487 (2010): 92–107.
Peterson, Christopher. "The Aping Apes of Poe and Wright: Race, Animality, and Mimicry in 'The Murders in the Rue Morgue' and *Native Son*." *New Literary History* 41 (2010): 151–71.
Poe, Edgar Allan. *Complete Tales and Poems*. Edison, NJ: Castle Books, 2002.
———. *The Detective Stories of Edgar Allan Poe*. Los Angeles: Sugar Skull Press, 2015.
Powers, David. *The Overstory*. New York: W. W. Norton and Company, 2018.
Rankine, Claudia. *Citizen: An American Lyric*. Minneapolis: Graywolf Press, 2014.
Reynolds, Davis S. *Faith in Fiction: The Emergence of Religious Literature in America*. Cambridge, MA: Harvard University Press, 1981.
———. "From Doctrine to Narrative: The Rise of Pulpit Storytelling in America." *American Quarterly* 32, no. 5 (Winter 1980): 479–98.

Selected Bibliography 85

——. *Mightier Than the Sword: "Uncle Tom's Cabin" and the Battle for America.* New York: Norton and Co., 2011.
Robbins, Hollis. "Harriet Beecher Stowe and 'The Man That Was a Thing.'" In *The Annotated Uncle Tom's Cabin*, edited by Henry Louis Gates Jr. and Hollis Robbins, xxxi–xlvii. New York: W. W. Norton, 2007.
Roy, Arundhati. "The Greater Common Good." In *The Cost of Living*, 1–90. New York: Modern Library, 1999.
——. "The Ladies Have Feelings, So . . . Shall We Leave It to the Experts?" In *Power Politics*, 1–33. Cambridge, MA: South End Press, 2001.
Russo, Mary. *The Female Grotesque: Risk, Excess, and Modernity.* New York: Routledge, 1994.
Scaggs, John. *Crime Fiction.* New Critical Idiom. London: Routledge, 2005.
Schade, Leah D. *Creation-Crisis Preaching: Ecology, Theology, and Preaching.* St. Louis: Chalice Press, 2015.
Scott, James C. *Domination and the Arts of Resistance: Hidden Transcripts.* New Haven, CT: Yale University Press, 1990.
Sigurdson, Ola. "The Christian Body as a Grotesque Body." In *Embodiment in Cognition and Culture*, edited by John Michael Krois et al., 243–58. Amsterdam: John Benjamins, 2007.
Solnit, Rebecca. *Hope in the Dark: Untold Histories, Wild Possibilities.* Third edition. Chicago: Haymarket Books, 2016.
Stowe, Harriet Beecher. *The Minister's Wooing.* Hartford, CT: Stowe-Day Foundation, 1988.
——. *Uncle Tom's Cabin.* Mineola, NY: Dover Publications, Dover Thrift Editions, 2005.
Stringfellow, William. *An Ethic for Christians and Other Aliens in a Strange Land.* 1973; reprint; Eugene, OR: Wipf and Stock, 2004.
Thunberg, Greta. "The Disarming Case to Act Right Now on Climate Change." TEDxStockholm, November 2018, https://www.ted.com/talks/greta_thunberg_the_disarming_case_to_act_right_now_on_climate/transcript?language=en#t-24447.
Tompkins, Jane. *Sensational Designs: The Cultural Work of American Fiction, 1790–1860.* New York: Oxford University Press, 1985.
Utych, Stephen M. "How Dehumanization Influences Attitudes toward Immigrants." *Political Research Quarterly* 71, no. 2 (2018): 440–52.
Wallace-Wells, David. *The Uninhabitable Earth: Life after Warming.* New York: Tim Dugan Books, 2019.
Welborn, L.L. *Paul, the Fool of Christ: A Study of 1 Corinthians 1–4 in the Comic-Philosophic Tradition.* Early Christianity in Context. London: T & T Clark, 2005.
Welch, Sharon D. *A Feminist Ethic of Risk.* Revised edition. Minneapolis: Fortress Press, 2000.
Wilson, Brittany. *Unmanly Men: Refigurations of Masculinity in Luke–Acts.* New York: Oxford University Press, 2015.
Woodyard, Kerith M. "Pussy Riot and the Holy Foolishness of Punk." *Rock Music Studies* 1, no. 3 (2014): 268–86.
Yuknavitch, Lidia. *The Book of Joan.* New York: HarperCollins, 2017.

Index

abolitionist movement, 18, 33, 36
   and antiabolitionists, 18
acronyms, 72–73
action
   decisive new, 69
   empathy and, 30
   hope and, 65–66, 68–69
   moving people to, 30
   for preachers, 22–24, 62–79
   See also specific topics, e.g., climate change/crisis
Africa, 74–75
African Americans, 15, 18–36, 53n43, 73
Akhmatova, Anna, 16
Alberta, Canada, 74
Alexamenos graffito, 7, 9, 37
"aliens," 20, 23
ambo, 51
America, 27. *See also* Central America; North America
American Jeremiad, The (Bercovitch), 26n29
anger
   weaponized grotesque used to create, 21
   See also rage
"animalistic dehumanization," 18–23, 37–38, 48, 70
anxiety
   sexual and economic, 18
   during times of change/transition, 20
   See also fear
apocalypse, xi, 59, 61, 64. *See also* climate change/crisis
apostasy, 12–14

Appalachia, 74
art/artists, xiii, 4–7, 43, 73. *See also individual names; specific titles/descriptions*
asylum seekers
   reduced to things, 21
   separation of families, 30, 72
   See also immigrants; refugees
atonement, 9, 11
"authorial voice" of the preacher, 69

Bakhtin, Mikhail, xiv, 6–7, 41–42, 46–47, 50, 76
   on dialogical truth, 56, 69n33
Baldwin, James, 33n54
baptism, 43
Barth, Karl, xiv
Bauerschmidt, Frederick, 50–51
beauty, 6–7, 12–15, 38–39, 43, 68n31
   destructive ideology of, 31–32
Beecher, Henry Ward, 26–27
Beecher, Lyman, 26
Beecher Lectures, xv, 27
Bercovitch, Sacvan, 26n29
Bible
   used to support slavery, 30
   See also New Testament; Old Testament
binary patterns/categories, 6, 12, 37, 41, 47–49
birth, 46
   of Jesus, 44–45
   new, 51
   See also rebirth
Black Lives Matter, 20
Blackwater (Ekman), 1

blasphemy, 43, 52
bleeding woman, 48–50, 56–57
Bluest Eye, The (Morrison), 31–32
bodily functions, 42, 44. *See also* lower body
body/bodies
  classical, 47
  daily realities of, 42, 44
  environmental, 76–79
  grotesque, 46–57
  leaky, 48–50, 54, 76, 78
  margins of, 47–50, 55, 76
  porous, x, 48–50, 54, 56, 76
  See also lower body
Body of Christ (church), grotesque, xiv, 51, 54–56, 79
Bonhoeffer, Dietrich, 68
boundaries, 46–50, 54–55, 69, 76
Bowler, Kate, 3–4
Brooks, Phillips, 27
Brown, Alexandra, 8
Brown, Teresa Fry, 53n43
bureaucracy, 71–75
Bussie, Jacqueline, 10–13

Campbell, Charles, 32n51, 34–35
Canada, 29, 74
cancer, 3–4
"carbon offsets," 74n53
caricature, 19–20
carnival/the carnivalesque, x, xiii, 7n20, 41–57
caskets/hearts "locked down as the lids of caskets," 22, 24, 28, 32
Cassuto, Leonard, 19–20, 23
Central America, 14
Cha, Steph, 2, 19n10
change/transition, 54, 79
  perpetual, 55
  times of, 20
chaos, 2, 20n10
charity, 27
children in cages. *See* families, separation of

Christ. *See* Jesus Christ
Christian Imagination, The (Jennings), 11, 31–32, 36, 38, 79
Christianity, xiv, 43n8, 51, 54–56, 79. *See also* church; faith
Christian life, 10–11
  as perpetual transition, 55
Christmas, 44
Christology, 36, 38
church
  ecclesial hierarchies, 45, 52–54
  ecclesiology, 54
  grotesque Body of Christ, xiv, 51, 54–56, 79
  perpetual transition as character of, 55
Citizen: An American Lyric (Rankine), 15
classical body, 47
Clifton, Lucille, 35
climate change/crisis, 11, 59–76
  preaching and, 59n2, 62–79
closure, vi
Collins, Billy, xiv
Colón-Emeric, Edgardo, 14n45
colonialism, 31–33, 70, 74n53
  colonial narrative, 36
color, people of, 53n43, 70, 74–75
common good, "greater," 70–73, 75
Cone, James H., 38–39
confession, 30
conscience, 21–22, 36, 70
contradictions, x–xi, xiv, 5–8, 10–12, 15, 39, 64, 68
control, pleasure of, xi
conversion, 26
convict leasing, 19
corruption, challenging, 52
cosmos, 62, 78–79. *See also* creation
creation
  Jesus as firstborn of all, 78
  new, 11, 45, 63, 66
  solidarity with, 79
  See also cosmos; earth

Index

crime fiction, 2–3, 17, 19n10, 20
cross, the, 8–16, 37, 44–45, 50, 52
   and the climate crisis, 66
   and the lynching tree, 38–39
   as mystery, 39
   scandal of, 8, 39
   stations of, 15, 39, 45, 78
   theology of, 10
   See also crucifixion
Cross and the Lynching Tree, The
   (Cone), 38–39
cross-dressing, 47, 53
Crucified God, The (Moltmann), 14
crucifixion, 8–16, 38, 43–44, 68, 76,
   78. *See also* cross, the
cruelty, 28n37, 36, 75. *See also specific
   topics, e.g.,* families, separation
   of

Dante Alighieri, 16
Davis, Angela, 33–34
Davis, D. Diane, 10
death
   civic, 16
   the climate crisis and, 11
   of moral conscience/moral
     imagination, 22
   and rebirth, 10, 13, 15, 49, 55, 64, 79
   of system, 9
   weaponized grotesque as leading to,
     22–23
   See also specific topics, e.g., climate
     change; crucifixion; lynching
death of Jesus, 37–38. *See also* cross,
   the
defiance, holy, 44–45, 54
degradation, 41, 47
dehumanization, 18–20
   "animalistic dehumanization,"
     18–23, 37–38, 48, 70
   and the climate crisis, 70–76
   and humanizing stories, 28–35, 73
   people reduced to numbers (or non-
     statistics), 72

   people reduced to things, 21, 36–39,
     70
   rhetoric of, 20–21, 23, 70–73
   "uninhabitants," 72
   the weaponized grotesque and,
     70–76
Denysenko, Nicholas, 51–54
deregulation, 60
despair, 4, 67
Diallo, Amadou, 22
dialogue, 54, 56–57
   listening, 13, 57
   truth, dialogical, 56, 69n33
Dietschy, Nathalie, 43nn8–9
dignity, 73
disabled people, 20, 50
discipleship, 12
   homiletical, 57
"discombobulating juxtapositions," 9
discovery, 10, 13, 15, 49, 55, 64, 79
disgust, 8, 21
displacement, 60, 63, 70–76
disruption, xi, 2–4, 10, 20, 37, 49, 55,
   64, 66–68
divinity, 8, 49
doctrine, 3, 8–11, 27
   from doctrine to narrative, 27
dogma, 31
dominant social order, 9, 19–20, 24
Dostoevsky, Fyodor, 56, 69n33
double-bind, 32
Douglas, Ann, 26
Douglass, Frederick, 24, 33n53
"The Dream of a Ridiculous Man"
   (Dostoevsky), 56
droughts, 61, 74–75

earth, 7, 41, 45
   the climate crisis (environmental
     grotesque), 59–79
   Eaarth (McKibben), 61–62
   environmental justice, 69–76
   new, 63
   See also creation

Index

ecclesiology, 54
economic order, 69
   the climate crisis and, 61
Ekman, Kerstin, 1–2
elites. *See* power/the powerful
El Salvador (San Salvador chapel), 14–15, 39, 45, 78
emotions, 29–34
   and people reduced to things, 21
empathy, 30, 34
Endo, Shusaku, 12–13
enslavement. *See* slavery
environmental body, 76–79
environmental grotesque, 59–79
   preaching and, 64–79
environmental justice, 69–76
eschatology, 50
Eucharist, 51
euphemisms, 72–73
Europe, 33, 70, 74
Everything Happens for a Reason and Other Lies I've Loved (Bowler), 3–4
exclusion/the excluded, 7, 43–44, 54–55, 70
extinction, 60, 76
Exxon Valdez, 74

faith, 11–14, 27
   and apostasy, 12–14
   emerging from scandal of the cross, 39
   See also Christianity
false patterns, 2–5, 12, 23, 32–35, 38, 44, 55
families, separation of
   immigrant, 30, 72
   no official figures kept of/reduced to non-statistics, 72
   people in prison, 21
   slave, 21, 29–31, 33
   at the U.S. border, 30, 72
fascination, 7–10, 49n8

fear
   on part of those in power, 19
   weaponized grotesque used to create, 21
   See also anxiety; terror
Feast of Fools, 53
feelings. *See* emotions
feminism, 52, 54
fiction, popular, 24–27
   women novelists, 25–28
"firstborn of all creation," 78
First Reformed (film), 67–68
flesh
   the term, 78
   See also body/bodies; Word, Incarnate
Florence, Anna Carter, 15–16
foolishness, xiii
   Feast of Fools, 53
   foolish wisdom, 8
   holy fools, 53
forgiveness, 37, 67–68
fossil fuel industry/extraction, 59, 63, 73–74
Fram, John, 19n10
France, 53
freedom, xi–xii, 45
French, Tana, vi, 2n3, 3n5
Fugitive Slave Act, 24
fumie, 12–13

gender, xi, 8, 48–49
glaciers, melting, 61
globalization, 75
global warming, 11, 59–75
"global weirding," 62
God
   "just out of focus, just beyond the reach of language," 55–56
   living, 68
   Word of, Incarnate, 41–57, 78
goodness, 7
good news ("Where is the good news?"), 3

gospel
   folly of, xiii
   as grotesque, 1–16
   interval of, 64
   preaching a grotesque, 11–16
   role of popular fiction in spreading, 27
   See also preaching
Gospels, 44, 48, 50, 76
grace, divine, 66, 68
graffiti, Roman, 7, 9, 37
Great Awakening, 26
"The Greater Common Good" (Roy), 70–73, 75
"green colonialism," 74n53
Grimaud, Hélène, xiii
grotesque, the, 5–6, 8
   carnivalesque, 41–57
   degradation, as engaging in, 41, 47
   history of, 6
   instability of, 23
   laughter, grotesque, 9–10, 70–71
   as liminal, 23
   realism, grotesque, 41–46
   scandal of, 56
   See also Body of Christ (church), grotesque; environmental grotesque; weaponized grotesque; *specific topics, e.g.,* hope: grotesque
grotesque body, 46–54
   preaching, homiletics and, 54–57
grotesque gospel, 1–16
   preaching, 11–16
grotto, 1, 5–8, 76–77

Harpham, Geoffrey, 10
Harrisville, Roy, 9
hearts "locked down as the lids of caskets," 22, 24, 28, 32
heaven, 4, 7, 41, 45, 62, 78
   new, 63
Hedrick, Joan D., 24n22

hierarchies, 45
   ecclesial, 45, 52–54
   political, 54
   social, 18–20
histories ("No, stop, they have histories!"), 22–23, 30–31
"holy defiance." *See* defiance, holy
Holy Spirit, 14
homiletics, xiv–xv, 57
   homiletical novels, popular, 27
   human-centered, challenge to, 76–79
   "New Homiletic," the term, 28
   women novelists and, 25–28
   See also preachers; preaching; *specific topics and individual names, e.g.,* grotesque body; Stowe, Harriet Beecher
hope, 10, 39
   and action, 65–66, 68–69
   cheap/misguided Christian, 63, 67–68
   the climate crisis and, 64–69
   grotesque, 64–69
hopelessness, 68n31
horror, 2n3, 7, 9–10, 18, 38
human-centered homiletic, challenge to, 76–79
humanizing stories, 28-35, 73
human life. *See* life/human lives
humor. *See* laughter, grotesque
hybrids/hybrid forms, 6, 52
   hybrid life, Christian life as, 10–11
Hyde, Lewis, 44

identity, 26n29, 54–55, 77
   displacement and, 70
illness, serious, 3–4
imagination, 77
   The Christian Imagination (Jennings), 11, 31–32, 36, 38, 79
   homiletical, xiv–xv
   moral, death of, 22
   "unimagined communities," 71
   the weaponized grotesque and, 71

Immersion (Piss Christ) (Andres Serrano's photograph), 43–44
immigrants
  separation of families, 30, 72
  treated as things, 21
  Trump's language for, 20–21
  See also asylum seekers; refugees
imprisonment
  convict leasing, 19
  for-profit prisons, 21
  mass incarceration, 19
  prisoners as slaves, 21
  prisoners reduced to numbers/things, 21
  of Pussy Riot members, 52
Incarnate Word, 41–57, 78
incarnation, "deep," 77–78
incongruities, 5–11, 13, 23–24, 37–38, 41, 55, 57, 64, 69, 71, 77
India, 70, 72–75
indigenous people, 20, 74n53. *See also* displacement
inequality, 75
insanity, 10, 13, 15, 49, 55, 64, 79
insects, and climate change, 61, 63, 65
Intergovernmental Panel on Climate Change, 60
interruptions/interrupting
  openness to, 55–57
  preachers interrupting the weaponized grotesque that leads to death, 22–23, 62–79
  rhetoric of, 71
  the status quo, 9, 11, 29, 39, 45, 53, 66–68, 77
  the weaponized grotesque, 23
intersectionality, 73n51
interval of the gospel, 64
"Introduction to Poetry" (Collins), xiv

Japan, 12
Japanese Americans, 20
Jennings, Willie James, ix–xii, 11, 31–32, 36, 38, 79

jeremiad, 26
jesters, xiii
Jesus Christ
  birth of, 44–45
  Body of Christ, grotesque, xiv, 51, 54–56, 79
  death of, 37–38
  depicting people as Christ figures, 37n71
  "firstborn of all creation," 78
  Incarnate Word, 41–57, 78
  as leaking power, 48–50
  Resurrection of, 14, 50, 76, 78
  See also cross, the; crucifixion; specific topics, e.g., *Uncle Tom's Cabin* (Stowe): Tom as Christ figure
Jewish people, 20
Joel, prophecy of, 65–69
Johnson, Elizabeth A., 77–78
jokes, crucifixion, 9
Judd, Wynona, 45
justice
  environmental, 69–76
  for the poor, 14
justice system, 19n10

Kavanaugh, Brett, 20
Kelley, Mary, 26
kenosis, 14
Klein, Naomi, 61–62, 69, 73–74
knowledge, system of, 23
Kuryluk, Ewa, 6–7

language
  God "just out of focus, just beyond the reach of language," 55–56
  new homiletical, 79
  vulgar, 52
  See also rhetoric; stories/storytelling; *specific topics, e.g.,* immigrants
laughter, grotesque, 9–10, 70–71
leaky body, 48–50, 54, 76, 78

Index   93

"Let Them Drown: The Violence of Othering in a Warming World" (Klein), 73
LGBTQ+ people, 20–21, 52, 54
lies, 71
life, Christian. *See* Christian life
life/human lives, 3n5, 10–13, 42, 45, 75
   descriptions of, 15
   See also body/bodies; dehumanization; reality/realities; *specific topics, e.g.,* displacement
Life of Brian (Monty Python), 9
limitations, 25
Lincoln, Abraham, 28–29
Lippard, Lucy R., 43n8
Lischer, Richard, 9
listening, 13, 57
Lorensen, Marlene Ringgaard, 57n49, 69n33
lower body, 42–43, 45–46, 52
lynching, 38–39

Maddow, Rachel, 28
Magnificat, the, 44–45, 49, 54
"The Man with the Flow of Power: Porous Bodies in Mark 5:25-34" (Moss), 48
margins/the marginalized, 45–50
   bodies, margins of, 47–50, 55, 76
   carnival as theology of, 45
Martinez, Demetria, 22–23, 30–31
martyrdom, 12, 14
Mary, 44–45, 49–52, 54
   "holy defiance" of, 44–45, 54
   Punk Prayer to (Pussy Riot), 51–52
Maslenitsa (Russian Orthodox carnival season), 51
mass incarceration, 19
McCracken, David, 5n10
McCray, Donyelle, 30n44, 47
McKibben, Bill, 61–62, 65–66
meanness, 69, 75
Memphis, sanitation workers in, 24
mercy, divine, 66

Merton, Thomas, 67
microaggressions, 15
Miller, Laura, 2n3
Minister's Wooing, The (Stowe), 26–27
Moltmann, Jürgen, 14
Monty Python, 9
Morrison, Toni, 31–32
Moss, Candida, 48–50
motherhood, 33–34
mountaintop removal, 74
Muir, John, 76
"The Murders in the Rue Morgue" (Poe), 17–19, 38
mystery genre, 2n3mystery/mysteries, 4–5, 43, 46
   cross as, 39
myths, 19, 38n72

narrative/narratives
   collision of, 29
   from doctrine to, 27
   resolution, 2
   See also stories/storytelling; *specific topics, e.g.,* colonialism
National Endowment for the Arts, 43
nationalism, 60
"national sacrifice areas," 74
nation-states, xi
Native Americans, 20
natural disasters
   people depicted as, 21, 75
   See also climate change/crisis
new heaven and new earth, 63
"New Homiletic," the term, 28
New Testament, 8–9. *See also* Gospels
Niger Delta, Africa, 74
Nixon, Rob, 71n40
norms/normativity, xi, 5–8, 10, 33, 37, 41, 47–50, 55. *See also* status quo
North America, 74. *See also* Canada; United States
novels, popular, 24–28
   homiletical, 27
   women novelists, 25–28

94   Index

numbers, humans reduced to, 21, 72
   and non-statistics (no figures kept), 72

Obama, Barack, 20
Obama, Michelle, 20
objectification, 20–21. *See also* dehumanization
O'Connor, Flannery, 4–5
oil spills, 74
Old Testament, 26
opposites, 17
   destabilizing pairings of, 8, 10, 37, 42, 49
oppressive systems/ideology, 7, 23, 35, 38
orangutan, 18–19
order, 2, 14, 19
   economic and political, current, 69
   old, 45
   "rage for," 12, 43–44, 55
   restoration of, 3, 19–20
   social, 9, 19–20, 24
   See also disruption
Orr, Gregory, 4, 38
"othering," 73
outrage, 24, 28, 33
Overstory, The (Powers), 60–61, 68n31, 77

PAPS ("Project-Affected People"), 72
paradox, 4–6, 8–10, 13, 15, 41, 43, 48–49, 55, 66
Paris Climate Accord, 74
particularity, scandal of, 56
passion narrative, 36
patriarchy, xi
patterns
   binary, 12
   death of, 9
   neat, comfortable, 68
   new, 79
   See also false patterns; *specific topics, e.g.,* disruption

Paul, xiii, 8–9, 42
performance, 45, 48, 57. *See also specific topics/descriptions, e.g.,* carnival/the carnivalesque; Pussy Riot
persecution, 12, 16
Phelps, Elizabeth Stuart, 28
Philadelphia, 18–19
Piss Christ (Andres Serrano's photograph), 43–44
Poe, Edgar Allan, 7, 17–19
poems/poetry, xiv, 12, 15–16, 22, 31, 35, 57. *See also individual poets; specific poem titles*
police brutality, 19n10, 22
political hierarchies, 54
political order, 69
political power, 19–21, 60
political rhetoric, dehumanizing, 20–21
polyphonic approach to preaching, 57, 69
poor people
   the climate crisis and, 70–73
   justice for, 14
porous bodies/boundaries, x, 48–50, 54, 56, 76
Portugal, 12, 30–31
Powers, David, 60–61, 68n31, 77
power/the powerful, 8, 55, 75
   and absurd claims/lies, 71
   carnival and, 45, 53
   and conscience, 70
   divine, 49
   dominant social order, 9, 19–20, 24
   fear on part of those in, 19
   and "greater common good," 75
   Jesus as leaking power, 48–50
   political, 19–21, 60
   and times of change/transition, 20
   weak, 8, 49–50, 76
   and weaponization of the grotesque, 70
   See also specific topics, e.g., climate change/crisis; colonialism

prayer, 7
   Punk Prayer (Pussy Riot), 51–52
preachers, ix–xv
   "authorial voice" of, 69
   as called to speak a counter-rhetoric, 23
   crime novelists and, 3
   of the fictional page, 25–28
   and humanizing stories, 28–35
   interrupting the weaponized grotesque that leads to death, 22–24, 62–79
   kenosis of, 14
   resisting the weaponized grotesque, 17–39, 62–79
   women, 25, 50
   women novelists as, 25–28
preaching, ix–xv
   the challenge for, 8
   and the climate crisis, 59n2, 62–79
   as grotesque, 55–57
   a grotesque gospel, 11–16
   history of, 25
   polyphonic approach to, 57, 69
   pulpit storytelling, 27
   See also homiletics; stories/storytelling; *specific topics, e.g.,* dialogue; grotesque body
pride, 67
prisons. *See* imprisonment
propaganda, 34
   and pressure on preachers, xi
prophets, Old Testament, 26. *See also* Joel, prophecy of
protest fiction, 24
protestors, 20, 52, 54
Punk Prayer (Pussy Riot), 51–52
Pussy Riot, 51–54
Putin, Vladimir, 51–54

race, origins of, 36
racial gaze, 38
"racial grotesque," 20
racialism, 24nn22–23

racial tension, 18–19
Rachmaninov's *Vigil,* 52
racism, 15, 19, 24, 30–33, 74
   theology and, 36
rage, 4, 30
   "rage for order," 12, 43–44, 55
   See also anger
Rankine, Claudia, 15
"ratiocination," 17–18
realism, grotesque, 41–46
reality/realities, 2n5, 8, 11, 15, 26, 32n51, 48
   bodily, 42, 44
   of global warming, 61
   imagination and, 39
   See also truth; *specific topics, e.g.,* climate change/crisis
rebirth, 10, 13, 15, 49, 55, 64, 79
redemption, 11, 15, 78
redemptive suffering, 38
refugees
   due to climate change, 61, 75
   rhetorical dehumanization of, 75
   separation of families, 30, 72
   See also asylum seekers; displacement; immigrants
repentance, 66, 69
repulsiveness, 7–10, 38, 43
Requiem (Akhmatova), 16
resistance/resisting the weaponized grotesque, 17–39
   first step of, 23
   preachers and, 22–24, 62–79
respectability, xi
Resurrection of Jesus, 14, 50, 76, 78
revelation, 10, 13, 15, 49, 55, 64, 79
revival movement, 26
revolution, 25n23, 45
revulsion, 7–10, 38, 43
Reynolds, David S., 25n24, 27
rhetoric
   absurd claims/lies, 71
   acronyms, 72–73
   counter-rhetoric, 23, 73

rhetoric (*continued*)
  dehumanizing, 20–21, 23, 70–73
  euphemisms, 72–73
  statistics (or non-statistics), 72–73
  See also dialogue; language; *specific topics, e.g.,* refugees
righteousness, 12
Rodrigues, (Father) Sebastian, 12–13
Roman graffiti, 7, 9, 37
"romantic racialism," 24n22
Romero, Óscar, Saint, 14, 44
Roy, Arundhati, 70–73, 75
rubble/revelation, 10, 13, 15, 49, 55, 64, 79
Russia, 51–54
Russian Orthodox Church, 51–54
Russo, Mary, 47–50

sacrifice
  "sacrifice zones," 74–75
  sacrificial theology, 38
  See also cross, the
Said, Edward, 73
salvation, 26n29, 39
San Salvador chapel, 14–15, 39, 45, 78
Scaggs, John, 19n10
scandal, xiii–xiv, 5, 10–11, 13, 24, 37, 42–43, 52–53
  of the cross, 8, 39
  of the grotesque, 56
Schade, Leah D., 59n2
Schrader, Paul, 67–68
sea level rise, 63, 74–75, 79
"secular answer," 67–68
separation of families. *See* families, separation of
sermons
  grotesque, xv
  mock, 42–43, 54
  See also homiletics; preaching
Serrano, Andres, 43–44
shame, 12, 53
Silence (Endo), 12–13
sinfulness, 12

slavery
  families, separation of, 21, 29–31, 33
  post-slavery era of convict leasing, 19
  prisoners reduced to, 21
  system of, 24, 28, 30
  See also abolitionist movement; *Uncle Tom's Cabin* (Stowe)
Smith, Christine, 30
social hierarchies, 18–21
  dominant social order, 9, 19–21, 24
social justice, 14
solidarity, 39, 78–79
soteriology, 38n72
Soviet Union, 16
Stalin, Joseph, 16
stations of the cross, 15, 39, 45, 78
statistics, 72–73
status quo, 6, 19, 29, 45, 52–53.
  See also norms/normativity; *specific topics, e.g.,* hierarchies
stereotypes, 30n44
Stevens, Wallace, 12
stories/storytelling
  counter-rhetoric, importance of, 23, 73
  danger of telling another person's/of misrepresentation, 33–35
  and hearts "locked down as the lids of caskets," 22, 24, 28, 32
  histories ("No, stop, they have histories!"), 22–23, 30–31
  humanizing, 28–35, 73
  pulpit storytelling, 27
  See also preaching
Stowe, Harriet Beecher, 24–30, 32–34, 36–38
strength
  and weakness, 12–13
  See also power/the powerful
"submergence zones," 72, 74

Index

suffering, 11–13, 16, 44, 62, 71, 78
   redemptive, 38
   See also specific topics, e.g.,
      crucifixion
suicide, 29, 67
Surin, Kenneth, 11
"Sweating, Spitting, and Cursing: Intimations of the Sacred" (McCray), 47
sympathy, 32–33
system/systems
   death of, 9
   See also under specific topics, e.g.,
      slavery: system of

tar sands, 74
tears, 30–32, 44
terror, 7, 9, 12, 16–17. *See also* fear; *specific topics, e.g.,* crime fiction
theology
   carnival and, 42–43, 45
   the challenge for, 8
   folk, 45
   grotesque gospel and, 11
   and racism, 36
   sacrificial, 38
things, people reduced to, 21, 38, 70
   Jesus, 36–39
This Changes Everything (Klein), 61–62
Thunberg, Greta, 59, 65–66
Toller, (Rev.) Ernst, 67–68
Tompkins, Jane, 26, 37n71, 38n72
torture, 12–13, 15. *See also specific topics, e.g.,* crucifixion
transfiguration, 14
transition. *See* change/transition
tricksters, xiii
Trump, Donald, 20–21
Trump, Eric, 20
truth
   dialogical, 56, 69n33
   at the edges, 57
   openness to, 56–57
   See also reality/realities

Truth, Sojourner, 23–24
Tuckerman, Henry, 27
Twain, Mark, 27
types, avoiding treating people as, 35, 37n71

ugliness, 13, 18, 24, 31, 69
Uncle Tom's Cabin (Stowe), 24–26, 28–30, 33
   Tom as Christ figure, 36–39
Underground Railroad, The (Whitehead), 34
"unimagined communities," 71
"uninhabitants," 72
United States, 19n9, 20–21, 24n23, 30, 32n51, 36. *See also specific topics and events*

violence, 11, 15, 25n23
   "slow violence" of climate change, 63
vocation, 13, 26

Warner, Susan, 28
Warren, Robert Penn, 4
weakness
   strength and, 12–13
   weak power, 8, 49–50, 76
weaponized grotesque, 17–39, 69–75
   antidote to, 30
   bureaucratic, 71–75
   current reassertion of, 21
   death, as leading to, 22–23
   false patterns of, 23
   instability of, 23
   political rhetoric as reasserting, 20–21
   preachers, and interrupting/resisting, 22–24, 62–79
   resisting, 17–39, 62–79
white gaze, 28, 33–34
Whitehead, Colson, 34
whiteness, 20, 31, 70
white supremacy, xi, 20

Index

"why some people be mad at me sometime" (Clifton), 35
wisdom, 8, 67
   foolish, 8
witness, Joel's, 67–69
women
   and the carnivalesque grotesque, 49–50
   dehumanization of, 20–21
   novelists, 25–28
   preachers, 25, 50
   See also individual names/descriptions, e.g., bleeding woman; Stowe, Harriet Beecher; *specific topics, e.g.,* motherhood; slavery

Word, Incarnate, 41–57, 78
Word before the Powers, The: An Ethic of Preaching (Campbell), 32n51
Word on the Street, The (Saunders and Campbell), 34–35
works righteousness, 68
World War II, 20

Yezhov, Nikolai, 16
young people, 54
Yuknavitch, Lidia, 79n69

Zurara, 30–31, 36

www.ingramcontent.com/pod-product-compliance
Lightning Source LLC
Chambersburg PA
CBHW030301010526
44107CB00053B/1773